16 Melville on Melville

Melville on Melville

edited by Rui Nogueira

London

Secker and Warburg in association with the
British Film Institute

The Cinema One Series is published by
Secker and Warburg
14 Carlisle Street, Soho Square, London W1V 6NN
in association with *Sight and Sound*
and the Education Department of the
British Film Institute, 81 Dean Street, London W1V 6AA

General Editors
Penelope Houston and David Wilson (*Sight and Sound*)
Christopher Williams (Education Department)

Melville on Melville by Rui Nogueira
first published by Secker and Warburg 1971
is a *Sight and Sound* publication translated and edited by Tom Milne
Copyright © 1971 Rui Nogueira

ISBN 436 09920 9 (hardcover)
ISBN 436 09921 7 (paperback)

Designed by Bentley/Farrell/Burnett

Printed in Great Britain by
Jarrold & Sons Limited, Norwich

Contents

Cover: Jean-Pierre Melville (photograph by Nicoletta Zalaffi)

Introduction

First of all – since you've asked me to introduce the book by
saying what I think of it, and since my comments are likely to
be not so much an introduction as an introductory conclusion
– I think it's still too soon to draw any real conclusions from
my twenty-five years of professional activity. I also think that
this posterity I sometimes think about is a problematic thing
because there are so many films made. It's crazy to think that
we've reached a point where the number of films produced in
America is a quarter of what it used to be thirty years ago;
all the same, the thousand or so films produced throughout
the world, year in and year out, gradually pile up and bury the
ones made before just a little bit deeper.

I was very glad to see that the authors of *30 Ans de Cinéma
Américain* share my tastes. I think I am the last living witness
in France who can testify on behalf of that pre-war American
cinema. One day I shall no longer be around, and there will be
no one left in France with a memory like mine who can really
assess these films as they deserve. Because if you see them now
at the Cinémathèque, you can't place them in the context of
the year in which they were made. The film which was released
in April 1934 – between March 1934 and May 1934 – isn't
at all the same thing when you see it now some afternoon or
evening at the Cinémathèque. So: are my films – and I'm not
putting on a false modesty act here – worth talking about in

Les Enfants Terribles: Cocteau and Melville as extras in the train sequence the same terms as some of these other films I'm always talking about? I don't know the answer, and nobody will until some fifty years from now when the Henri Langlois Panthéon has been replaced by a definitive Panthéon . . . because I don't accept the Langlois Panthéon, which is subjective, distorted, and to be approached with caution. What I *do* accept, of course, is Langlois' mission, his life-work, and the Cinémathèque, that marvellous invention he shares with Franju. But the films Langlois loves – there I can't agree with him.

Anyway, since this is supposed to be an introduction, by way of introduction I'd like to say what a film-maker should be. A film-maker should be a man constantly open, constantly traumatizable; his sense of observation must be as highly developed as possible, and his sense of psychology; he must have exceptionally keen visual and auditory perception . . . and a memory. Because what people often assume to be imagination in my films is really memory, things I have noticed walking down the street or being with people – transposed, of course, because I have a horror of showing things I have actually experienced. A film-maker must be a witness of his times. If, for instance, all my films were to be shown in some sort of seminar fifty years from now, people must be able to feel that they add up to something, that the first and last film undoubtedly have something in common, that they talk the same language and about the same thing, whether the stories are invented or taken from existing sources, that it's the same mind behind them, the same man with the same colours on his palette. The tragic thing, for me, is when a creator suddenly makes a radical change in his way of talking about things, because this means that one of his two formulas – maybe the new one, maybe the old – is wrong. So the essential thing is that there must be an intrinsic resemblance between the first film and the last. I don't know if this is as true in my case as I should like; but to me the ideal creator (a term I prefer to director or *auteur*, because the French don't have a good word for what we are, or at least

8

what I am, since more and more I enjoy writing *and* directing) is a man who has created an exemplary body of work, one which can serve as an example. I don't mean an example of virtue or quality. I don't mean that you should be able to say 'You see? He's exemplary because everything he did is admirable' – rather that everything he did can easily be summed up in a couple of hundred words to explain what he has done and who he was.

I think one must be free, courageous, intransigent – and healthy. That, alas, is the first commandment: 'Thou shalt have health.' I was made very much aware of this during *Le Cercle Rouge*: the film-maker must be in perfect physical shape because he's like the Volga boatmen hauling their boats; he has to drag an entire crew in his wake. So when the time comes for a film-maker and he's a tired old gentleman, he'd better just put down his camera and prune his roses. There are roses in my garden, but I shan't be pruning them. I haven't the time just now.

1 : 'Civilization! Civilization!'

The basic principle of this book is precisely the same as Truffaut's Hitchcock. *But do you think a creative film-maker like Hitchcock is honest when he explains how he achieved particular effects?*

No, never! Hitchcock is marvellously two-faced. He feels – and he is certainly right – that you shouldn't hand out the recipes for dishes you make better than anyone else. The secret ingredient is a sacred thing. A painter doesn't disclose the mixture of blue and grey he used to obtain a particular tone of sky. I don't think a creator, a genuine creator, really wants to cheapen things that have taken him long years to learn. A film-maker is like the master of a shadow-show. He works in the dark. He creates through 'effects'. I am perfectly aware of the extraordinary dishonesty it takes to be effective; but the spectator must never be allowed to realize the extent to which everything is manipulated. He must be spellbound, a prisoner, in a state of submission.

For you, a film-maker is first and foremost an entertainer. When and how did you become interested in the world of entertainment?

I came to it in early childhood through reading plays which were published with photographic illustrations in the series 'La Petite Illustration'. Then I became fascinated by the circus, and after that, the music-hall.

L'Aîné des Ferchaux: Melville demonstrating (for Jean-Paul Belmondo) the attack on Todd Martin

There was a wonderful place in Paris – the Empire, in the Avenue de Wagram – where all the great international music-hall stars appeared: Al Jolson, Jackie Coogan and his father, Sophie Tucker, Ted Lewis, Harry Pilcer, Jack Smith, Jack Hylton and so on. I went there constantly, as well as to the Casino de Paris and the Folies Bergère, with an uncle who was a personal friend of Maurice Chevalier, Mistinguett and Josephine Baker. *That* was entertainment!

Music-hall was a thing of perfection. At that time it interested me much more than the cinema because it was endowed with words and music. In the same way, theatre pleased me because it had *language*. Cinema only came third. When I used to go to the local cinema of an afternoon, it was of course to see silent films, and I felt extraordinarily frustrated. The first film that really made an impression on me was *White Shadows in the South Seas*, by Van Dyke and Flaherty, in which Monte Blue uttered the first words ever spoken on the screen: 'Civilization! Civilization!' That was at the Cinéma Madeleine in 1928, well before *The Jazz Singer*.

At that time you had already made several 9·5 mm films?

I got my first camera, a hand-cranked Pathé Baby, in January 1924. So I was six years old. My first film was about the Chaussée d'Antin – where we were living at the time – as seen from my window. You could see the Cadum Baby, cars passing by, a little dog with St Vitus's dance belonging to a lady who lived across the street . . . everything I could see from my window, in fact. But I soon realized that I wasn't in the least interested by the films I made. I much preferred other people's. So I very quickly got tired of my Pathé Baby. On the other hand, I never tired of my Pathé Baby projector, because it let me see any film in the world in my own home. The Pathé Baby catalogue of films for hire, a vast catalogue with a plot synopsis and still for each film, was the most beautiful thing in the world. There were Westerns, all of

Lino Ventura and Melville during the shooting of *Le Deuxième Souffle*

Keaton's films, Harold Lloyd's, Harry Langdon's, Chaplin's . . . you hired them from a photographer, Sartoni. So every week I was able to see four or five new films, either two, three, or four-reelers. It was *l'amour fou*, completely. The basis of my cinematographic culture.

From time to time I went on filming people in the street, still without enthusiasm, until my twelfth birthday, when I was given a 16 mm camera. But I preferred being a spectator. With the coming of sound, the mania had really begun: my days began at 9 a.m. in a cinema (the Paramount), and ended the same way at 3 a.m. the next morning. The pull was stronger than anything else. I couldn't shake off this absolute *need* to absorb films, films and more films all the time.

Did your formation, the development of your taste, come through films?

Yes, but four people had a real influence on me: my parents, my older brother and my uncle.

My father, who was a wholesale merchant, was a very witty, intelligent man. A humorist in the Jules Renard manner. That is a thing of the past, men have no humour any more.

My uncle was a big Paris antique-dealer, at a time when that was a real profession. I was a very small boy when he made me understand one day the difference between things that are beautiful and things that are less so. I was asking him why the enormous difference in price between two objects in his shop, and he took two apparently identical Louis XIV armchairs and said: 'You see, here are two more or less similar armchairs. Yet one is worth more than the other. Look at them carefully so you make no mistake, then tell me which is the more beautiful and therefore the more expensive.' I looked at them carefully, I thought hard, and I made no mistake. Pleased, my uncle then added, 'From now on, throughout your life, you will always know the difference between what is beautiful and what is not.' I have never forgotten that lesson. So I believe I have very sound taste. For instance, at this moment we are watching *Written on the Wind* on television. It's a pleasant film, very well made, but it's not a great film although Douglas Sirk did make one remarkable film, *A Time to Love and a Time to Die*. The actress in it, on the other hand – Dorothy Malone – is a very fine piece of Louis XIV furniture. I think we are agreed about that, but if by any chance you were to disagree with me, well, it is I who would be right.

In that case, how does it happen that your celebrated list of sixty-three pre-war American directors does not include the names of Chaplin, Walsh or De Mille?

At that time the American cinema comprised a famous trinity: Capra, Ford and Wyler. I am not talking here about our tastes, but of their genuine importance in the cinematographic hierarchy of the period. But for a director to be included in my list, all that was necessary was that he should have made one film, just one, which I loved. I did not include Chaplin because he is God, and therefore beyond classification. I drew up that list, which relates only to the sound era, after much careful research and a great deal of thought and critical analysis:

Lloyd Bacon, Busby Berkeley, Richard Boleslavski, Frank Borzage, Clarence Brown, Harold S. Bucquet, Frank Capra, Jack Conway, Merian C. Cooper, John Cromwell, James Cruze, George Cukor, Michael Curtiz, William Dieterle, Allan Dwan, Ray Enright, George Fitzmaurice, Robert Flaherty, Victor Fleming, John Ford, Sidney Franklin, Tay Garnett, Edmund Goulding, Alfred Green, Edward Griffith, Henry Hathaway, Howard Hawks, Ben Hecht, Garson Kanin, William Keighley, Henry King, Henry Koster, Gregory LaCava, Fritz Lang, Sidney Lanfield, Mitchell Leisen, Robert Z. Leonard, Mervyn LeRoy, Frank Lloyd, Ernst Lubitsch, Leo McCarey, Norman Z. McLeod, Rouben Mamoulian, Archie Mayo, Lewis Milestone, Elliot Nugent, Henry C. Potter, Gregory Ratoff, Roy del Ruth, Mark Sandrich, Alfred Santell, Ernest Schoedsack, John M. Stahl, Josef von Sternberg, George Stevens, Norman Taurog, Richard Thorpe, W. S. Van Dyke, King Vidor, William Wellman, James Whale, Sam Wood, William Wyler.

Now, as it happens, I didn't like any of Walsh's pre-war films, because they were all marginal and they all had something wrong. Take my word for it, Walsh is a poor film-maker. It is tragic to see how far young critics can be deceived, how much influence one kid can have on a whole generation. I am thinking of Pierre Rissient. He thought Walsh had talent, he said so, and he has said it so often that a kind of religion has sprung up in Paris with people worshipping Walsh. The only Walsh film I ever liked was *Objective Burma!*, which he made in 1945. I would have to see it again before being definite about it, because it may well not stand up now.

I have never seen a completely successful De Mille film

either. I believe, and I thought so even more after seeing *Sunset Boulevard*, that De Mille was above all an actor, a brilliant actor. The problem is that he was never a real director, like all actors who – unlike Orson Welles – become directors merely by chance.

Have you ever thought of making a new list of sixty-three post-war directors?

Yes, it ought to be done, although I don't think one could find sixty-three important new directors. The war turned everything upside-down, you know. A whole world disappeared, making way for another which is still in a state of formation. Thirty years ago, let's say, in May 1939 to be precise, a certain form of civilization suddenly disappeared along with a certain form of cinema. It was quite remarkable. When I arrived in London in 1943, I saw twenty-seven films during my week's leave, and I quickly realized that the cinema had changed. Even a comedy like H. C. Potter's *Mr Lucky*, with Cary Grant and Laraine Day, no longer had the same tone. The tempo, the pace of the pre-war comedies had disappeared. Although they hadn't yet or were only just entering the lists, one already felt in the air directors like Welles, Kazan, Wilder, Wise, Preminger, Mankiewicz, people who really came out of the American cinema. It was in London that I discovered a whole transatlantic cinema I did not know. I'm not talking about *Gone With the Wind*, which did resemble the pre-war cinema, but about the other twenty-six films made between 1942 and 1943. In London, the cinema and the world took a new turning for me.

So it wasn't your encounter with Clark Gable in a London shirtmaker's that marked this rupture with the past?

Everything was magical in those days, especially in the latter half of the war. I was in English uniform, in transit in London for a few days, and I had the feeling that we were going to win the war. Suddenly de Gaulle's words to Colonel Passy in 1942 became overwhelmingly true and swept away the feeling of defeat which one could still sense in France, where I had come from: 'Basically, the war is over. Now it is merely a matter of attending to the formalities.'

Gripped by this sensation of victory, and yoked to this monstrous American and Allied force, what more natural than suddenly to see God in person? The fact that a few days previously I had seen Clark Gable in *Gone With the Wind*, without a wrinkle or a white hair, in no way affected the charm of this man lined by the sun and more than silvery at the temples, whom I recognized by the sound of his voice before I saw him and he flashed his teeth at me in a smile.

You know, I can recall almost all the events in my life from 1930 to 1940 sandwiched between two films, because I remember the order in which I saw them. Sometimes I say to old friends from before the war: 'You remember? That was between *Three Comrades* and *Wuthering Heights*.' The American films of that time were landmarks in our lives.

Were you fond of the pre-war French directors?

Fond, yes, but I didn't love them. To love, one must be madly in love. All the same, Prévert, Carné and Jeanson undoubtedly represented a very fine kind of cinema. I remember one film in particular which I adored when it came out was Carné's *Le Jour se Lève*. I still say 'Carné's', because at the time when these films impressed me I was not yet aware of the role played by Prévert. Now I know that the credit should go to Prévert. Carné was merely a good entrepreneur; the spine, the skeleton, story, dialogue, casting, that was Prévert. At the same time one must not underestimate Carné's 'Hollywood' quality as a director, because Carné, you see, could very well have worked in Hollywood with scripts written by someone else. In my list of sixty-three directors, for instance, there were at least forty who were just Carnés, so it's not a thing to be sneezed at.

No, I did not love the French cinema of my youth, which is why I fell back on Hollywood. As a matter of fact, even today when one says 'French cinema', it has an oddly pejorative taste in both mouth and mind.

Born Jean-Pierre Grumbach, you changed your name to Jean-Pierre Melville. Why?

Through pure admiration and a desire to identify myself with an author, an artist, who meant more to me than any other.

Three American writers left their mark on my adolescence: Poe, London, and of course Melville. When one is young, one never knows exactly what one's own mythology will be as an adult. Today, Melville and London are *ex aequo* for me. I discovered Melville, long before Jean Giono's translation of *Moby Dick*, by reading in English *Pierre: or the Ambiguities*, a book which left its mark on me for ever.

I took the name of Melville well before I started in films: I went through the war with it. Once the war was over and I wanted to call myself Grumbach again, I realized that it was impossible in practice to turn the clock back. Apart from the fact that I was known to hundreds of people by the name of Melville, that was how I was listed on my military papers. I was even decorated under the name of Melville . . .

2 : 'My Original Sin'

When you were demobilized in November 1945, you wanted to begin directing films. So you became your own producer . . .

After the war, I applied to the Technicians' Union for an assistant-probationer's card (*assistant-stagiaire*). I was interviewed by Marc Maurette and René Lucot, who told me that I had to produce evidence of a job first. But to get a job one had to be qualified, and the qualification was the union card. Lack of a card was sufficient reason to withhold permission for employment. Do you realize just how far the Communist dictatorship went? I mean Communist, not union, since the cinema trade union was already entirely in the hands of a man I like very much and who has certainly changed since, much more than he dares admit: Louis Daquin.

In order to combat this vicious circle, I founded my own production company. Actually, I saw Daquin again very recently during the shooting of *L'Armée des Ombres*, and he confessed that he had been wrong. The moment a man tells you 'I was wrong', I think he is completely, absolutely pardoned for his wrongs. Daquin caused me a good deal of misery at one time, but maybe it was good that I had to fight against men like Daquin and Autant-Lara. If they have changed, I have changed too. If Autant-Lara and Daquin have come a long way towards my position of 1947 – I'm not talking about politics, of course – I have gone a long way towards their exclusivist position. Well, as we all know, exclusivism is Fascism. I hate saying this, but I must: nowadays, I wonder if one should not be a little more difficult about the question of qualification. When you think that every year there are between fifty and sixty new directors, it makes you shudder. The cinema is a sacred thing no longer. Of course everyone has the right to become a film-maker, but not to make just anything, any old how. The disturbing thing today – I am a member of the Commission de Censure and I see films which should never have been made – is that the Centre National de la Cinématographie may give fifty million old francs to a young director to make something absolutely indescribable. So the question I ask myself is this: 'When Daquin and Autant-Lara opposed me with such violence and force, with powers they would certainly no longer command today, were they perhaps not right in a way?' In other words, I was a sorcerer's apprentice. I said that everyone has the right to make a film – and I still think so today – and now the cinema is suffering the consequences. I believe you must be madly in love with the cinema to create films. You also need a huge cinematic baggage. In 1947 I was unbeatable, and I'm not just talking about technique; I knew everything, even the credit titles by heart. I have always learned cinema, I have never ceased to learn cinema.

How did you come to make your first film, the only short of your career, Vingt Quatre Heures de la Vie d'un Clown?

One of my first passions, well before the cinema, was the circus. Out of this passion, a friendship was born: with the clown Bèby. Bresson had made a very attractive film, *Les Affaires Publiques*, in which Bèby was something of a predecessor to Chaplin in *The Great Dictator*. I wanted to take the first plunge with a homage to Bèby, the last of the great clowns, which would stand as a sort of testimony to an

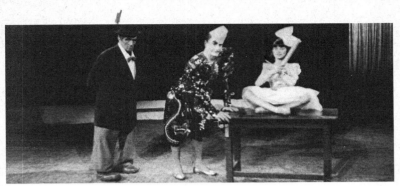

Vingt Quatre Heures de la Vie d'un Clown

art which was about to disappear. Unfortunately I bungled it completely, and it was my own fault . . . This was in 1946, the war had just ended, and raw stock was scarce. To buy it you had to have coupons, so I bought some 1942 Agfa stock on the black market. I don't know if you realize what four years does to black and white stock? It's fantastic! The film was fogged by age, and there was nothing one could do about it. Then, when it came to synchronizing the sound – I had to shoot it silent because of lack of funds – I discovered that Bèby couldn't read. I had to do the synchronization word by word, which means that I had to tamper with the montage. The result was so monstrous, such a horror, that I shoved it all away in a cupboard with the intention of leaving it there forever. One day Pierre Braunberger asked me if I hadn't made anything before *Le Silence de la Mer*, and I let out that I had made this terrible short. He was so insistent about seeing it that in the end I showed it to him. The worst of it was that he liked the film and persuaded me to let him have it, although I laid down my conditions: the removal of my name from the credits, the soundtrack . . . everything. He told me recently that he had made a lot of money out of the film.

Vingt Quatre Heures de la Vie d'un Clown is something I would like to be able to forget. It's the error of my youth, my original sin. You can't run away from it!

3 : Le Silence de la Mer

For your first feature, you chose to adapt the Vercors story, Le Silence de la Mer. *How and when did you get the idea of making this film?*

From the day I was given the Vercors story to read by Jean-Paul de Dadelsen, the Alsatian poet who was killed in the war, I was absolutely determined that it would be my first film. It was in English and was called *Put Out the Light*. That was in 1943.

A little later I got in touch with *France Libre* to ask for the rights, and as luck would have it the man responsible was J. Pierre-Bloch, one of General de Gaulle's future Ministers and a childhood friend of mine, at that time aide to Colonel Passy. When he told me that Louis Jouvet had just sent a request for permission to film it from South America, I said: 'But you have no right to decide, you don't even know who Vercors is! Legally, you are laying yourself open to a whole heap of trouble.' I was even devious enough to revive the arguments of Ilya Ehrenburg, who had said that the book was 'a work of provocation, certainly written by a Nazi to support the Gestapo's insidious propaganda campaign . . .' I was so persuasive that in the end Pierre-Bloch withheld permission from Jouvet, who wanted to play the role of Werner von Ebrennac because there is a phrase in the book which reads:

'. . . I noticed his surprising resemblance to the actor Louis Jouvet.'

Why was Vercors subsequently unwilling to let you have the rights to his book?

We discussed the matter, in an exchange of letters in which he told me his refusal was prompted by the fact that *Le Silence de la Mer* was part of the French national heritage. Maître Arrighi, who had been head of the Resistance, had asked him never to sell the rights, for he viewed with horror the idea that this story, which had virtually served as a Bible during the war, might be made into a film. This view, moreover, was held unanimously by all members of the Resistance. Faced with Vercors' refusal, I finally said to him: 'All right, I'll make a film for my own private use.' The reply to that wasn't long in coming: 'I refuse to authorize that either.' In the end I gave a written guarantee to submit the film as soon as it was finished to a jury of Resistants selected and assembled by Vercors. Should one single member of this jury be opposed to the film being shown, I pledged myself to burn the negative.

Did the fact that you were obliged to wait until 1947 before starting to shoot Le Silence de la Mer *enable you to make use of your own production company?*

My production company did me no good, for three reasons: (1) I had not obtained the rights to the book. (2) I had no director's union card because I did not wish to be unionized. (3) I had no right to 'coupons' for film stock, being 'unqualified' professionally. So the freedom of my personal position automatically debarred me from any assistance, financial or otherwise.

So you then shot Le Silence de la Mer *clandestinely, without either authorization or assistance, completely outside the production system of the time?*

23

Le Silence de la Mer: Jean-Marie Robain (*left*) and Howard Vernon

Well, I did manage to find one source of assistance, only one, but absolutely indispensable: the laboratory. I was lucky enough to happen on a Resistant, Monsieur Colling, then Director of the GTC laboratories, who said to me: 'Monsieur Melville, I have faith in you. Make the film. If Monsieur Vercors still withholds the rights when it is finished, well, you can owe me the money and pay me back some day.' He didn't even ask me for security . . . nothing! This man helped me enormously and I can never say so enough.

I started the film on 11 August 1947, twenty-seven days shooting in all. I would work only when I had collected enough money to pay the hire of equipment and my only electrician-grip; the bus which took us to Vercors' house; Decaë and my cast. I always insisted that people should be paid as we shot, so there were twenty-seven separate payments. We were not insured, so that had an accident occurred during shooting I would never have been able to finish the film.

How did you find your cast?

For the role of the uncle, I had in mind Jean-Marie Robain, a wartime comrade I had lost touch with. One day I met him quite by chance in the street where I lived and where, by a strange coincidence, he lived too. This sort of countersign is conclusive: Robain got the part!

As for Howard Vernon, I had seen him as my character ever since seeing him in a Henri Calef film, *Jéricho*, although there were a lot of German actors in Paris at the time. Nicole Stéphane was a family friend. One day she told me of her desire to become a director, and I said: 'The day I make a film, you shall become my assistant – although I would prefer you to act in it.' Her absolutely pure profile and limpid eyes were perfect for the role of the niece.

Why did you want to make the film in Vercors' own house?

Because it was there that Vercors imagined this story on a basis of reality. A German officer who limped and played tennis as therapy for his leg had actually lived in his house. No *rapport* grew up between them, but Vercors had noticed that this officer was rather unusual, for his room was not only full of books which bore witness to his exceptional culture, but contained a bust of Pascal instead of Hitler's portrait.

Starting from there, Vercors had translated the story into poetic terms. Thus his wife became his niece, for instance, to permit the introduction of a sublime love theme.

On the first day of shooting, Vercors and his wife were away. It was Emmanuel d'Astier, to whom they had lent the house, who opened the door to us. To my 'Good morning, Monsieur le Ministre,' he replied with regal disdain, 'Oh! it's you . . . the Cinema.' And he went away to sit in the garden, paying not the slightest attention to us for the rest of the day.

The last day of shooting was another matter. Vercors' wife, who had returned earlier than expected, flew into a rage at seeing the upheaval we had caused in her home. Her exact words were, 'Monsieur, this house has known the German, but the German, at least, respected it.' To which I replied, 'But the German, Madame, was not a film-maker.'

Basically, all I needed was a room thirteen by sixteen feet, so I could have shot in the studio or in a house of the same type nearer Paris; but I preferred the real thing, even though I knew it would give me no particular pull with the jury.

Although it was you who discovered Decaë with Le Silence de la Mer, *he wasn't on the film from the beginning?*

No, I began shooting with Luc Mirot. He did the summer scene where Howard Vernon comes in with a tennis racquet under his arm, and also the one at the end in Vernon's room when he is getting dressed, ready to leave. When we were shooting this scene, Luc Mirot didn't want to light the shot as I asked. When I insisted, he argued: 'If I light it your way, you'll get crap.' 'I want crap,' I said. The next day I sacked him. After that I had another cameraman, André Vilar, but that didn't work out either.

That was how I met Henri Decaë, a young man as sympathetic as he was shy, gifted with great intelligence, and exactly sharing my tastes for all things cinema. The first day we worked together was very pleasant, the second, delightful. From the third day onwards the die was cast. We got on so well that we did everything together: shooting, editing, dubbing and mixing.

In spite of your complete fidelity to the book in both letter and spirit, you turned it into a very personal work, avoiding all the pitfalls of 'filmed theatre'.

The thing I liked enormously about *Le Silence de la Mer* was

26

the anti-cinematographic aspect of the story, which immediately made me think of making an anti-cinematographic film. I wanted to attempt a language composed entirely of images and sounds, and from which movement and action would be more or less banished. So I conceived the film a little like an opera. Afterwards . . . well, the result wasn't too bad because there have been a lot of films since . . . I sometimes read (I am thinking of the reviews after *Le Samourai* and *L'Armée des Ombres* came out), 'Melville is being Bressonian.' I'm sorry, but it's Bresson who has always been Melvillian. Take a look at *Les Anges du Péché* and *Les Dames du Bois de Boulogne*, and you will see that they aren't yet Bressonian. Look at *Le Journal d'un Curé de Campagne*, on the other hand, and you will see that it's Melville. *Le Journal d'un Curé de Campagne* is *Le Silence de la Mer*! Some of the shots are identical. The one, for instance, in which Claude Laydu is waiting for the train on the railway platform is the same as the scene with Howard Vernon in my film. And the voice-off of the narrator, of the man who is telling the story? As a matter of fact Bresson did not deny it when André Bazin put it to him one day that he had been influenced by me. All this has been forgotten since.

Without in any way breaking the unity of the story, you added two sequences which were not in the book. The first of these is the meeting in the snow between Howard Vernon and Nicole Stéphane.

I wanted to give my characters every possible opportunity to recognize their love. One possibility, not offered by the book, was this meeting out in the open, free from the presence of any witness. They might have stopped and talked to each other, she might have looked at him and smiled . . . which couldn't have happened inside the house because both niece and uncle were prisoners of the attitude they had adopted from the beginning, on the day of the German's arrival, and she couldn't change in her uncle's presence.

Le Silence de la Mer: The meeting in the snow (Nicole Stéphane and Howard Vernon)

To film this encounter, for your reverse angles you used a fix-focus shot for Nicole Stéphane and a track for Howard Vernon. Why?

Because he is walking towards her wanting to *do* something, whereas she is holding herself in check. But a director's reasons should remain more or less imperceptible to the spectator. Whenever the spectator becomes aware of a director's intentions, the rhythm of the film is inevitably broken.

The slight trembling of the image in the shots of Howard Vernon, on the other hand, was caused by an aberration in the camera. It was turning too quickly. I had to slow down the action by duplicating every third frame, but it still jerks. That was in no way intentional, although it would be easy enough now for me to invent some directorial justification.

The second added sequence is the one near the end, when Vernon finds the newspaper open at the words : 'It is a noble thing for a soldier to disobey a criminal order.'

That was to express the uncle's attempt to reclaim this man whom he was beginning to find sympathetic. He wants to make him understand, still without addressing him directly, that there is still time for him to opt out. For the scene I used the page of *l'Humanité* on which Anatole France's phrase was published at the time of the Marty and Tillon affair. These two French sailors had formented revolt on board their ship in the Black Sea by disobeying their commander's orders to bombard the Red Armies. Wonderful, isn't it?

Did you have any difficulty filming in the streets of Paris with Howard Vernon in German uniform?

We were liable to find ourselves being beaten up at any moment, because of course only two years earlier the Germans were still there. Most of the time I drove Vernon by car, put him down in the street, and rapidly took shots which corresponded exactly to the stock shots I had already chosen for the reverse angles. But there were moments when I had to do some directing; for instance, the enfilade of the rue de Rivoli with the two German sentries outside the Hôtel Continental. We snatched those shots, under constant threat of trouble.

Those shots serve to illustrate Vernon's descriptions of his two leaves in Paris. The first time, one can see no other German on the streets.

The first time Vernon goes to Paris you see no Germans because *he* doesn't notice them. You mustn't forget that he is German himself, so his compatriots don't bother him. For him, the revelation of the Occupation and its consequences comes only after the soirée spent with his comrades. It is in telling about his second leave, after this flash of conscience, that he says there were Germans in the streets and that you see those Germans.

For the shots in the Kommandantur, I used the office which had actually served the purpose, so as to have the view of the Opéra from the window. We were very close to events, so a semblance of realism was necessary both about the Germans and the Occupation. Today such details would be of little importance, but we couldn't just make it all up.

There is a phrase in the book which you kept in the film and which might have been written by you: 'Even were he my enemy, I cannot without compunction offend a man.'

Absolutely! Why does one choose a book? Because it contains situations and phrases which are a part of one, part of one's life. There are many things in the Gerbier of *L'Armée des Ombres* which are mine, and there is no doubt that had I been a priest, I would have been a priest in the Léon Morin mould. But I go further than Vercors: 'I offend no man.' I think the only way to achieve respect – and I wish to be respected – is to have supreme respect for others.

Another phrase you kept comes when the uncle's voice is heard off, saying: 'My niece had covered her shoulders with a printed silk square on which ten weird hands designed by Jean Cocteau gestured languidly at each other.' Is the fact that Vercors made this reference to Cocteau, whose Enfants Terribles *you were to adapt as your next film, another of those countersigns which led you to cast Jean-Marie Robain in* Le Silence de la Mer?

Yes, it was a way of tying things up. I knew Cocteau very well, and I greatly admired his work. I drew the hands on the cloth myself, and when Cocteau saw the film, he was intrigued to know where I had managed to find the scarf. He thought it was his work!

30

During the breakfast scene in the kitchen, one can see saucepans on the stove in the foreground, behind them the uncle and his niece drinking their coffee, and in the background, the German talking. Yet everything is in perfect focus.

At that time everyone was wondering how Orson Welles had done certain shots in *Citizen Kane*,[1] notably the one of Dorothy Comingore's suicide attempt. You saw the bottle of Gardenal in the foreground with the glass, Orson Welles coming into the room in the background, and between them the face and body of the dying Dorothy Comingore. But only she was out of focus! Opinions about how he achieved the effect were more than mixed. People were even talking of a special lens with two focal lengths and one of the components moving for a forty-eighth of a second so that the human eye had the impression that the foreground and background were sharp, etc., etc. In other words, a load of rubbish, incredible nonsense. Of course Welles never explained how Gregg Toland had done it, because he never denied that he owed the whole technical side of the film to Toland . . . but after seeing the film innumerable times, I came to the conclusion that he shot this sequence as a composite. So I decided to try it out myself. I began by doing a shot of the two saucepans with lights on them and a black cloth behind. Then I ran the film back and I removed the black cloth. The unlighted saucepans then masked what had already been recorded. The only trouble was that we had a couple of accidents. First, Decaë inadvertently picked up one of the saucepans, thus creating a moment of panic and suspense: if you look carefully, one of the saucepans has two handles because we didn't quite get it back in the same place. Then, once again, the camera began turning at the wrong speed (15 frames a second instead of 24), which meant that the movements of the characters were too rapid. So I had to make the actors move and talk – because Vernon speaks in the scene – in slow motion to compensate for the slow-motion camera.

1. *Citizen Kane* was not released in France until after the war.   31

We had problem after problem during the shooting of the film. For instance, we used nineteen different kinds of stock, from Rochester to Agfa by way of Kodak Vincennes. Now, while Rochester took eighteen minutes to develop, the Vincennes took nine minutes. We were continually getting lost in all these calculations, and were in constant danger of ruining the negative. But by the end of *Le Silence de la Mer* I had learned a lot: among other things, to be classical and not to try to revolutionize the cinema. I have never wanted to reinvent the cinema, and I continue to detest all those inventions which are rediscovered at regular intervals. The thing I dislike about these efforts is that they are almost always the work of amateurs, whether gifted or not, rarely of professionals. For a professional, the older he gets the more classical he becomes, the more anxious he is to respect form. If he doesn't do that, he is no professional.

Le Silence de la Mer is the work of a professional, even if well-known professionals of the time – who have completely disappeared since – described the film as 'amateur stuff'.

Can we return to the way you handled the story? The only time one hears the sounds of war is when Howard Vernon is describing Chartres Cathedral. You see the Cathedral, the camera pans to the right and discovers the mouth of a cannon, which fires five times.

In that pan, I start on the view of Chartres Cathedral, lift to the sky, and come down again to the mouth of a cannon on a tank which never moved from the Ecole Militaire in Paris, where it is still vegetating peacefully to this day. To fuse the sky of Chartres and the sky of Paris, I used a dissolve during the pan. It's actually Paris when you see Vernon giving the order 'Feuer!'

And how did you shoot the scene in the café with the patronne *serving behind the bar?*

Le Silence de la Mer: The café 'not open to Jews' (Howard Vernon)

I shot it in a café I had scouted carefully in a little village near Paris. First of all I told Decaë to take up his position and not to be surprised at anything that might happen. Then, while I was telling the *patronne* not to worry, I manœuvred the door of a telephone booth to which I had pinned a placard I had ready with the words, 'Not open to Jews.' At that point Howard Vernon was already in position for the shot, and I said to the *patronne*, 'We'll only be a moment, Madame, you'll see. All you have to do is give Monsieur Vernon his change.' I asked clients who wanted to leave to be patient for a minute, called 'Roll 'em', and the scene was in the bag. It was all over in a couple of minutes. Because we were in such a hurry, all you can read on the placard is 'Not open to J', but it was essential that the *patronne* should have no idea what we were up to. At that time the so-called Nouvelle Vague movement was still a long way off.

33

While you were shooting, you were also editing the film with Decaë?

That wasn't easy . . . Although we shot consecutively for the last three days of our schedule – notably the sequence in the German officers' club – many scenes which seem to follow each other in continuity were shot six months apart. There were even retakes, because sometimes I wasn't satisfied with what I had done before. Decaë and I did the editing from 35 mm nitrate rushes in my hotel room, where Decaë had set up his old Contin-Souza. We projected on to the wall. The machine used to get so heated that whenever we stopped it, the frame which was frozen would burn out and we'd have to replace it with a blank frame, bearing in mind that it represented an image to be used. We never could afford to have our rushes projected. The film would be delivered to us in the evening, and sitting on the bed I would look with the naked eye at what we had shot the day before. For a year – the happiest year of my life, I must admit – we were reduced to total penury. But it was a wonderful sensation, the feeling of creating something important while at the same time being so poor. It's ridiculous, what I'm about to say, but so very true: you do not need hope to venture, nor success to persevere. You see, my motto has always been 'Because I do not know what is impossible, I did it.' To tell you the truth, I did have moments of discouragement when I used to wonder if I was completely crazy – that was the general cry, 'Melville is completely crazy, he'll never finish his film' – to persist on a course which nobody could see leading anywhere. It was the first time anyone had tried to oppose the syndicalist structure of the French industry, as omnipresent and dictatorial as it is the world over. It took courage, you must admit, to stand firm to the very end without letting oneself be intimidated by every conceivable kind of threat and criticism. The CGT even had the gall to accuse us of making a film with Rothschild money because I had cast Nicole Stéphane as the niece, and she was

34

a Rothschild!

When I finished my film, in recognition of my efforts . . . I was fined fifty thousand francs by the Centre National de la Cinématographie. Can you imagine? Nowadays the CNC is likely to give the same sum as an advance on receipts to help someone set up a film. As I hadn't a penny, I managed to have the fine reduced to five thousand francs, and then a few years later to get a refund of four thousand francs. I sometimes feel like writing to them just for a joke to ask: 'Since you would now give me fifty thousand francs to make that film, can I please have my one thousand francs back?'

When Le Silence de la Mer *was finished, you screened it for a jury as agreed, and they had no objection to its being shown. But Vercors accused you of having invited the entire Parisian Press to this first screening, which was supposed to have been a secret one . . .*

In fact I didn't invite anyone. That's not my style. But I had asked George Cravenne, who wasn't yet well known, to arrange the screening for me at the Studio des Champs-Elysées, and I was as surprised as anyone to discover that he had invited everybody who was anybody in Paris. Even Noël Coward was there, on a flying visit to the capital. I was furious and wanted to throw everybody out, when Vercors spoke in a tone I didn't care for. So I thought, 'To hell with it, they're here, let them stay.' Cocteau was there, Mauriac . . . in other words, there was a top-drawer audience that October afternoon in 1948. Then Vercors decided to make a declaration of war on the Press . . . a declaration he had prepared in advance, of incredible stupidity. I assure you I was more dead than alive.

The jury voted 'Yes' unanimously . . . or almost.

I still have the voting papers of all twenty-four people involved. I had printed the name of each member on his paper, but at the last minute, since one of them was unable to come and we had been obliged to find a substitute, his paper was replaced by another with the name typed on. The only 'No' came from the heir to this paper who, in handing his vote to Vercors, had added: 'I am not the sort of person you ask at the last moment to make up a fourth at bridge,' and to whom Vercors replied, 'Very well, I won't count your vote.' That member was Pierre Brisson of *Le Figaro*, who died a few years ago.

With all these problems, you managed to get the film shown on what was then the most important circuit, and included the Gaumont-Palace and Rex.

Once the film was finished, I had to find a distributor. As I have always thought it better to go straight to God instead of to his saints, I decided to offer it to M-G-M. I therefore asked to see Mr King, who was the big boss for Europe, an intelligent American, well informed about France, and I said to him: 'I am just completing a film which I have made almost single-handed. It isn't in the least cinematographic, because there is no dialogue: one character speaks, and the other two listen ...' At that point he interrupted me with, 'Oh! what a wonderful picture!' 'Excuse me, Mr King,' I said, 'I haven't told you yet what it's about.' 'No, but I know ... you have been filming *Le Silence de la Mer*.' Extraordinary, wasn't it?

Pierre Braunberger, who had heard about this meeting, came to see me and managed to persuade me to give him the film. I made a silly mistake there! When it came to getting the film shown, I went to see Jean Hellman, owner of one of the biggest cinemas in Paris, the Rex, which worked in tandem with the Gaumont-Palace. He saw the film and loved it. Gaumont then threatened, 'If you show this film, our marriage is off.' To which Jean Hellman replied, 'All right, so the marriage is off.' Bernard Wibeaux, who was in charge of programming for the Gaumont, didn't back down either. He showed *Le Silence de la Mer* at the Gaumont as well. And it did very well ...

36

How much did the film cost?

Thirty thousand francs for the rights; thirty thousand to record the score with a hundred and twenty musicians; sixty thousand for everything else – a hundred and twenty thousand in all. At that time a film like Jean Delannoy's *La Symphonie Pastorale* cost one million francs.

If you had to remake it, would you do it differently?

Certainly. I think about the possibility sometimes, although I am terribly wary nowadays about the poetic side of the story. At that time I wasn't afraid of poetry in the cinema. Now it terrifies me. I realized that poetry in the cinema is dangerous the day André Gide saw my film. After all, Gide was a man well qualified to understand a story like *Le Silence de la Mer*, but he was terribly bothered by the girl's attitude. At the screening it was obvious that he wanted them to rush into each other's arms. Of course he was already very much in decline when he put himself out to come and see my film. The cinematographic side of it passed completely over his head. He couldn't even remember having read the book, which was odd because for a long time it was thought in London that Gide had written it, and as a matter of fact there are things in Vercors' work that are pure Gide. The influence is unmistakable. After the screening, the only thing he could find to say to me was: 'I think the girl was a fool. She deserved to be spanked.'

4 : Les Enfants Terribles

Like the boys in Les Enfants Terribles, *you were once a pupil at the Lycée Condorcet. Cocteau's novel was a great influence on your youth, wasn't it?*

No, let's keep this in proportion. Like all pupils of the Lycée Condorcet, I took part in those snowball fights in the Cité Monthiers, and we had all read *Les Enfants Terribles*. We considered it our book. But although I was very fond of the novel, the idea of making a film of it had never entered my mind.

Cocteau was a very cunning man. When he telephoned me the day after he saw *Le Silence de la Mer* to tell me he wanted me to film *Les Enfants Terribles*, he was not completely disinterested, as I might have thought at first . . . his admiration was sincere, but he also wanted to use me as a springboard for launching his new discovery, Edouard Dhermitte, whom he hoped to turn into another Jean Marais.

What were your relations with Cocteau?

Very, very good as long as I hadn't begun shooting; very, very bad as soon as I did begin.

I must admit that I wasn't at all easy at that time . . . I was very stubborn, with no taste for compromise. I was producer, director and adapter of the film – even though I did put

38

Les Enfants Terribles: Paul and Elizabeth in the sleeping-car (Nicole Stéphane, Edouard Dhermitte)

Cocteau's name on the credits as co-adapter – and I absolutely refused to be opposed, directed or controlled in any way. Now Cocteau, who had just completed *Orphée* and was at a loose end, came every day to watch me at work. On the first day of shooting, Dhermitte was doing a scene when he shouted, 'Oh no! Cut!' An icy silence fell like doom on the set. I can still remember the look of fright on Decaë's face as he edged quietly away from the camera. As for me, I just looked at Cocteau, who said hastily, and with an air of penitence, 'Forgive me, I don't know what came over me . . . I thought I was still on the *Orphée* set.' From that day on he never made the same mistake again. Sometimes he would try to . . . advise me, let us say . . . whereupon I would look at him dryly and say, 'No, Jean . . .' Our friendship suffered as a result.

You see, from the moment the affair had been set up and the advance received from the Gaumont Company, the one thing Cocteau wanted was for me to die so that he could make the film himself.

One day when I wasn't feeling quite up to the mark, I asked Cocteau to take over for the day. I sketched out for him all the shots I wanted him to do, making it quite clear that he was to follow my instructions exactly or do nothing at all. I need hardly add that he acquitted himself beautifully, exactly like an assistant. The shots were for the sequence we did at Montmorency, supposedly by the seaside, when Gérard's uncle buys himself the straw hat and Elizabeth and Paul force Gérard to steal a watering-can. Eight shots in all, which were supposed to be of a summer's day but were done in midwinter in the rain.

Cocteau was delighted, because he'd had *his* day of shooting.

I loved that man. He was intelligence, charm, talent itself . . . one of the real élite.

Do you feel that Les Enfants Terribles *suffers from problems of miscasting . . .?*

Of course. I would have liked a more fragile, more tender actor for the role of Paul, more ambiguous even. Edouard Dhermitte, with his great strength, left no room for ambiguity. Actually he was rather aware of this, and even had his hair bleached to try to identify with the character as much as possible. As for the rest of the cast, I am entirely responsible, although I now feel that Renée Cosima isn't too good in her double role. Nicole Stéphane, on the other hand, I think is absolutely extraordinary as Elizabeth. Her performance and her presence even makes one forget the absence of a Paul. As for Roger Gaillard, the delightful and very intelligent actor I chose to play Gérard's uncle, I thought then and I still think that he was wonderfully strange and funny. Even Cocteau, who was a little worried about my choice to begin with, was finally very happy with him.

Why do you think Nicole Stéphane never quite made it as an actress?

I don't know . . . She preferred being a producer, I think. Among other things, she has produced Rappeneau's *La Vie de Château*, and *Phèdre* for television. One day I would like to direct Cocteau's *Les Parents Terribles* on the stage, with her in the role played by Yvonne de Bray. I'm sure she would be fantastic.

Although you were obliged to give way to Cocteau on Edouard Dhermitte, you were able to use the music you wanted.

I had to give way on Dhermitte because it was in the contract, which is rather unusual where the assignment of rights is concerned. It was such a pity. He's a nice boy, and a painter of real talent. But I would much rather have had one of his paintings than have him in my cast.

As for the music, Cocteau wanted something in the style of Wiener and Doucet [a famous duo at the Bœuf sur le Toit just after the First World War] because he had written the book during his stay at the clinic for disintoxication at la Celle Saint-Cloud, while listening over and over again to the same record, 'Make Believe'. He was very anxious to use that, played on the piano, but I finally chose the music without even telling him. He still tried to force my hand a little, just a little, but he had an instinct for the right thing. 'One must always know just how far one has the right to go too far,' he used to say. Once the music had been recorded, he left it rather up in the air in his interviews as to who had made the choice, but since I went right on telling everybody it was I and I alone, he didn't insist. Eventually he said in André Fraigneau's book, *Entretiens autour du Cinématographe*, that he was very happy with the Bach music.

Were the costumes the only thing you brought up to date, then?

Yes. Originally I wanted to rejuvenate the film and set the action in 1925. But when Christian Bérard died, Cocteau begged me, 'Please don't set the film in 1925. Bébé is dead, and there is no one in Paris who could take his place.' In one way this was true: Bérard would have done marvellous sets and costumes. On the other hand, no one is irreplaceable . . . I preferred to leave the period undefined.

Although you designed the sets yourself, they were executed by Emile Mathys, weren't they?

You know, the problem with my films was that I never had enough people to list on the credits. Take Philippe Schwob, for instance, a distant cousin of mine and a designer by profession. On *Les Enfants Terribles*, where he was a tower of strength, he exercised the functions of production manager, location manager and property manager. Similarly, all the sets in the film were executed by one man, though designed by me. Yet some of them had to be constructed, even the

sleeping-car, which looks like the real thing but isn't. Emile
Mathys was a former anarchist and a craftsman of genius. I
have never found anyone quite like him since. He also played
a small part in *Les Enfants Terribles*, as the Vice-Principal of
the school.

*There is a remarkable shot in which Elizabeth looks at the photo-
graphs pinned to the wall in Paul's room — rather like the scene
where Howard Vernon surveys the living-room of the house in*
Le Silence de la Mer — *and we realize from her expression
that the photographs are all resemblances, more or less, of
Dargélos/Athalie.*

The photographs on the wall are of boxers, film stars and
gangsters who all look like Dargélos/Athalie. In an earlier shot
the camera had already prowled over the wall and the photographs, so I saw no point in doing it again. I thought it would
be much more interesting to give this feeling of discovering
the resemblance exclusively through Nicole Stéphane's expression. To prove that I am quite sincere when I say that I
have never invented a thing in the cinema, I'm going to tell
you the source for that scene. Some time after seeing the film,
people have the impression — as they have often told me — that
it was at this precise moment that they realized the resemblance between Dargélos/Athalie and the photographs. I
owe this false impression, if I have really brought it off, to
Orson Welles. Ages after seeing *The Magnificent Ambersons*, I
could still clearly recall the scene in which Joseph Cotten
walks with his daughter Anne Baxter in a garden of flowering
cotton trees. Well, do as I did and take another look at the film.
There's not a tree in sight, not even the shadow of a branch.
But they are talking about them, and I always remembered
that long, marvellous tracking shot which accompanies Cotten
and Baxter on their walk as taking place among trees in flower.
That's what cinema is all about! Once you have understood
that, you have made a beginning at least.

When Michael dies in his sports car, Cocteau's description corresponds almost exactly to the death of Isadora Duncan.

Precisely. I shot that scene near Ermenonville, which is quite close to the Mer de Sable. There are little pine trees like those on the Côte d'Azur and a forest exactly like the forests of the Midi. It was there I shot the sports car scene. After we had overturned it and damaged it a little, I wound Mike's scarf round the wheel, put a bit of smoke down, and spun the wheel so as to have Cocteau say that wonderful phrase: '. . . with this wheel turning slower and slower, like a lottery wheel.' Since I was my own producer, there was no question of going far from Paris to do this sort of shot.

In the last scene there is a remarkable crane effect. To get it, you used a lift, but one never for a moment suspects its existence.

At the time I had rented from the Société Nationale des Entreprises de Presse a very handsome office which had belonged to the proprietor of a pro-German newspaper, *Le Petit Parisien*, which was banned after the Liberation. It was in the hall outside this office that I shot the scene where Paul improvises a room out of screens, as well as the scene you mention. So as to be able to use the lift as a crane, I had made sure the lift shaft was never seen, simply by covering it with fabric. For the last scene I removed the fabric and put the camera in the lift, then took the lift up just at the moment when the screen collapses. I had also moved the room closer to the lift to heighten the effect.

As a matter of fact, there are other moments in the film where you might think I had used a crane, but it is actually the décor which moves. These were the scenes I shot at the Théâtre Pigalle, which was undoubtedly the finest theatre in the world. There were two seventy-two by one hundred and forty-four foot stages, which were actually six stages: one on top, another in the middle and a third underneath – all that

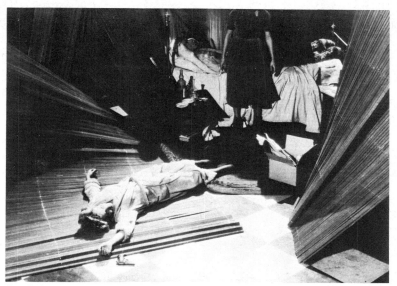

Les Enfants Terribles: The 'crane shot' when Elizabeth commits suicide (Nicole Stéphane, Renée Cosima)

twice over! Each stage moved up or down on three levels, and could also move forward or to the rear. When you see Jacques Bernard (Gérard) in the foreground while the room recedes behind him, he is on the forward fixed part of the stage while I move away the rear, mobile part of the same stage. At another moment, the camera is stationary above, but seems to move down towards the two beds: actually, it is the entire stage of the theatre moving up, a huge, monstrous lift, rising without a sound . . . At one point in the film, you see the theatre itself. I showed it to illustrate the line spoken by Cocteau in the commentary: 'The curtain rose on the drama of the room at eleven o'clock in the evening.'

You know, apart from the daytime exteriors, I shot the entire film at night, because I preferred sleeping during the day. At that time I was a Little Caesar, and I subjected the entire crew to this drudgery of working at night. I really was a

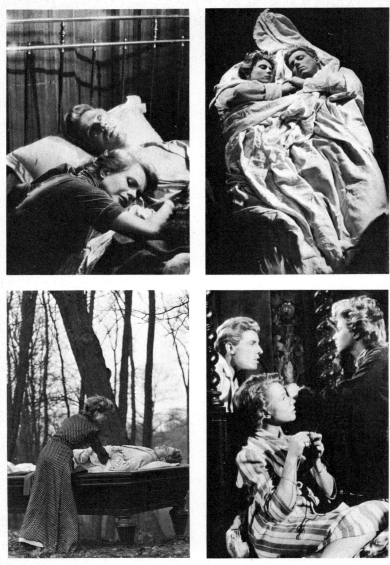

Les Enfants Terribles: Nicole Stéphane and Edouard Dhermitte with (*above left and below right*) Renée Cosima

night bird. Cocteau, poor man, wanted to be on hand to see that Dhermitte was getting on all right, but after about two or three o'clock in the morning he couldn't take it any more, and used to lie down on a high counter which was part of the décor and go to sleep there.

Some of the Nouvelle Vague directors – I am thinking particularly of Truffaut – liked Les Enfants Terribles *enormously.*

I know. When Truffaut was a novice film-maker, he was nice enough to tell me he had seen the film twenty-five times. He proved he knew it even better than I did. He not only knew the words, but the music which went with them. Chabrol knew *Les Enfants Terribles* very well, too. I know that when he was shooting *Les Cousins*, he said to Decaë, 'Here I want exactly what you did in *Les Enfants Terribles*.' That's why you can see absolutely identical camera movements in the two films.

In the scene in the dining-car, you can be seen with Jean Cocteau...

In my films I like preserving images and memories of my friends, of the people who have worked with me. During the scene on the platform at the Gare de Lyon in *Les Enfants Terribles* – the same platform where I have just done a sequence for *L'Armée des Ombres* – the voice announcing the departure of the train is that of my sound engineer, Jacques Gallois. And when Gérard's uncle speaks on the telephone to Paul's doctor, it is Cocteau's voice at the other end. For the commentary, spoken off, I also used Cocteau's voice because I thought it was marvellous. Such a beautiful voice deserves to be preserved. I am glad I did.

It is also Cocteau's heart beating when the doctor listens to Paul's chest. Since Dhermitte was supposed to be a sickly boy, I made Cocteau run round the auditorium before recording his heart so that it would be beating fast and hard.

47

5 : Quand Tu Liras Cette Lettre

Of all your films, Quand Tu Liras Cette Lettre *is the one you like least, or possibly not at all. Why did you make it?*

You know, when one makes films one doesn't like or doesn't believe in, one always tries to find excuses. The excuse I give myself for *Quand Tu Liras Cette Lettre* is that it gave me a chance to use Yvonne de Bray. Her brief appearance on the train is a joy to me.

However, the real reason for making the film was something else. In the terribly enclosed world of the French cinema in 1950, I was still thought of as an amateur, even a dilettante. I was always denied the status of professional, the most frequent reproach being that I was an intellectual and made intellectual films. I was reduced to despair by the realization that producers didn't have faith in me because, they said, I was much too intelligent to be a film-maker. One day Ray Ventura, who was a very important producer at the time, told me quite frankly: 'But Mr Melville, you obviously aren't a film director, because film directors shouldn't be intelligent!' I was so thrown by this that I decided people mustn't be allowed to think of me as intelligent or intellectual – which is far from proven anyway. They must be made to see once and for all that I was a showman, full stop. So I had to make a very conventional, very sensible film; a film within the system and not outside it. And that is why, from a very good script, admirably written by Jacques Deval, I made a film which could just as well have been made by any French director of the period.

But surely there are some sequences you like, some things that are Melville in it?

Yes . . . but only two or three things. Yvonne de Bray, first of all. Then, the scene of the first meeting between Yvonne Sanson and Philippe Lemaire, when she is getting petrol. I like the way Lemaire polishes the car, gradually getting closer until he brushes against Yvonne Sanson. There are also certain moments I quite like with Gréco as the nun . . . but it's not a good film.

Was the casting of Juliette Gréco part of your determination to be sensible, or was it simply a homage to the great days of Saint-Germain-des-Prés?

Oh, no, Juliette Gréco was the un-sensible side of the film. She was a good friend from the Saint-Germain days of '47, '48 and '49. At that time, I remember, I often went to the Club Saint-Germain where they had a band with fabulous musicians. It was there I had some marvellous times with Django Reinhardt. Nobody has written about Django better than James Jones in *From Here to Eternity*. Saint-Germain became something else after 1950, but before then . . . it was marvellous.

   Juliette Gréco has never really belonged in the film scene. Even during the time she was with Zanuck she wasn't part of that world. Zanuck himself couldn't impose her on the industry: you can't impose someone who won't belong. I was very fond of Juliette; she's an intelligent girl and a good friend. One day she got the idea of having her nose operated. She was right. In *Quand Tu Liras Cette Lettre* she is really beautiful. And when one remembers the chubby little thing of

Quand Tu Liras Cette Lettre: Irène Galter and Juliette Gréco

'47–'48 with that horrible big pointed nose . . . During *Quand Tu Liras Cette Lettre* she was so thin that I used to call her 'The Skate'.

In this film the Italian side of the co-production was represented by Yvonne Sanson and Irène Galter. You got on well with Irène Galter, but not, it seems, Yvonne Sanson?

I had accepted Yvonne Sanson because I thought she looked really beautiful in Alberto Lattuada's *Il Cappotto*. What I didn't know, however, was that she was Turkish. One often forgets that the Italians are the world's greatest experts in the art of dubbing, and they can therefore afford to use actors from any country in the world, even Turkey. Yvonne Sanson spoke only Turkish and a few words of Italian. The funny thing was that she claimed to be Greek and would only admit her origins as a last resort. So any sort of exchange, any understanding between us, was impossible. She was incapable of speaking her lines in French. So I would make her say anything. In a fit of exasperation I once even told her, 'Madame, say Bla-bla-bla,' and Philippe Lemaire had to play an entire scene with this woman who just went on saying 'bla-bla-bla' all the time. It was terrible. Afterwards, I got Nathalie Nerval to dub her.

But you had a French producer on the spot, hadn't you?

That's just it, he was never there. My producer, Monsieur Dubois, was a nice man – he is dead now, poor soul – but he didn't know anything about the cinema. However, he left me completely free to do absolutely anything I wanted. One thing I could never say about the film is that I suffered from an interfering producer. He never bothered himself about anything: I set the whole thing up myself. One day, after I had reproached him with never coming on the set and with taking no interest in the film, he finally did turn up at a screening of rushes and told me happily, 'You see, my boy, I've come along just to make you happy.' In the middle of the screening he suddenly cried out, 'Martini? What's that Martini ashtray doing there? You can't do that, my boy, you can't do that, I have a contract with Cinzano!'

Why did you use Henri Alekan as director of photography instead of Decaë?

The real reason I used Alekan is that Decaë was in love. It's fabulous, isn't it? Decaë had fallen in love with the girl who is now his wife, and at the time only one thing mattered to him: his fiancée. The day we did a test with Juliette Gréco, Decaë did everything in a terrific rush and the results were not very conclusive from a photographic point of view. Then, when the rushes of the test were screened he didn't even come to see them. I tried to smooth things out with Paul Temps, who was the production manager, but there was nothing to be done.

The end of the film brings it back full circle to the beginning with a long circular pan over the town and the convent . . .

The shot at the end is the one from the beginning . . . in reverse. I had the negative printed in reverse, frame by frame. The pigeons are even flying backwards, although you don't have time to notice.

And how did you shoot the scene of the accident in which Lemaire dies?

I shot that at the Gare de Varenne with Henri Tiquet, the greatest French camera operator of them all, at the camera. He'll never forget that scene, because he was so worried – Philippe Lemaire really did go under that train. He hung on to the buffer, then let himself be dragged along by the moving train, lifting his legs so as not to crush them. The scene was extremely dangerous, and Philippe Lemaire very courageous. At that precise moment, thinking he really had been crushed, Tiquet deserted the camera crying 'Aaaaaaaahhhhhhhh!' It fogged the end of the shot, since in those days you sighted through the film and the eye served as a stopper – but needless to say we didn't retake the scene.

Yvonne de Bray, who died shortly after appearing in the film, apparently gave you two precious pieces of advice about directing actors. What were they?

I can't tell you. You know, one is always more or less at war with actors, so . . . they mustn't know. Let's just say it's a secret.

6: Bob le Flambeur

In 1955, with Bob le Flambeur, *you shot your first original script.*

I had written *Bob le Flambeur* in 1950, five years before I filmed it. From my memories of a world I had known pretty well, I wanted to paint as truthful a picture as possible of the pre-war French *milieu*.

My original intention was to make a serious film, but after I had seen Huston's masterpiece *The Asphalt Jungle*, I realized I could no longer deal, either dramatically or tragically, with the preparation and execution of a robbery. So I decided to reshape my scenario completely and turn it into a light-hearted film. *Bob le Flambeur* is not a pure *policier*, but a comedy of manners.

Nevertheless it has echoes of Huston – the theme of the futility of effort.

True. Bob robs himself in blowing up the bank at the Casino. His beautifully prepared hold-up becomes completely unnecessary because he has just won the eight hundred millions in the Casino vaults by legal means. That's my taste for the absurd. There's still a bridge on the River Kwai nestling somewhere in my heart. I like futility of effort: the uphill road to failure is a very human thing. The scientists, for instance, are pushing research so far that there will inevitably come a moment when they can suddenly go no further. Man has conquered the moon and he wants to conquer every star in the solar system, but I think he will lose his bearings. Science is moving towards the moment of failure. In his progress from achievement to achievement, man comes inevitably to his last, absolute defeat: death.

Even so *Bob* is still a light-hearted film. Moreover, it ends on a pirouette. You remember, when Guy Decomble, the police inspector, says: 'With criminal intent and the job begun, it's five years right off. With a good lawyer and the job not started, you'll get away with three.' To which André Garret adds, 'And if you can get Floriot and Garçon, you might even be awarded costs and damages.' I thought it would be amusing to finish the film like that. It's funny to think that someone who has planned a hold-up and in a sense carried it out, may have nothing to fear from the law if he is defended by very good lawyers, and might even be able to claim damages.

All your films reveal a love of detail and of objects, which in-spired one critic to describe you as the Francis Ponge of the cinema. How do you feel about this?

It doesn't displease me, with the one reservation – and here I part company with the *nouveau roman* – that I don't like close-ups of objects. Objects are very important to me, but there is nothing like close-ups for dating a film. So, even if an object has real dramatic significance in a scene, I will place it any-where *except* the foreground. Hitchcock, of course, wouldn't hesitate to have a ringing telephone up against the camera if he has a corpse in the background; but I wouldn't do that.

What is the significance of mirrors in your films?

There is this moment of truth in all my films. A man before a mirror means a stock-taking. When he walks up the rue Pigalle at the beginning of the film, it's in front of a rusty mirror that Bob mutters to himself: 'A fine hoodlum face!' With this one phrase he sums up his entire life.

If I ever find my real *Bob*, you will be able to see the enormous difference that exists in the dialogue between the film I wrote and the film I made. The dialogue I had written rang true, like *Le Samourai*.

In that case why did you collaborate with Auguste Lebreton?

Well, I hadn't much to offer from the publicity angle. I wasn't well known, I had no stars. The fact that I was able to get a distributor and a guarantee was undoubtedly due to having my friend Lebreton's name on the credits. He was a top star that year because he had just had a huge success with *Du Rififi chez les Hommes* and *Razzia sur le Chnouf*, which were packing the audiences in. So I asked Auguste to do the adaptation and dialogue, and although he wrote some really fine stuff, he moulded it all to his own personal style. I can't look at *Bob le Flambeur* any more, and it is because of this dialogue, which has aged terribly. That's how it is: every time I collaborate with someone, something goes wrong. I have to work alone. The reason I still like *Les Enfants Terribles* is because the collaboration with Cocteau was limited to the book, and I condemned him to a total respect for the dialogue in the novel. Every time he tried to change something, I'd say, 'If you're going to write a new *Enfants Terribles*, I'm no longer interested in filming it.'

How did you choose your cast?

The first time I saw Isabelle Corey was in the Place de la Madeleine one day when I was driving past with my secretary after auditioning several girls for the part. Although she was twenty yards away on the other side of the road, I liked her at once. Since I couldn't leave the wheel or get close without making a difficult turn, I asked my secretary to go over and get her address. Instead she gave her my address, which was a bit tricky because she might very well never have telephoned me.

She had everything it takes to be a star, a big star . . . but she never knew it. She was fifteen years old, beautiful, intelligent. I had signed a long-term contract with her, but I must confess I didn't do much about taking her out or showing her off, because I hadn't the time. She suffered enormously as a result.

Then one day Isabelle came to ask me to let her play the second female lead in the Vadim film which Raoul Lévy was going to produce, *Et Dieu Créa la Femme*. I tried to dissuade her, telling her that Lévy would only have offered her the role in order to finish her completely because she represented a real threat to Brigitte Bardot. In the end, since she wouldn't listen to reason, I let her go, saying, 'A contract is something you can't explain. If you don't understand what it means, there is no longer any reason for it to exist.' I think I was right, because a few years later Isabelle Corey came to ask me to take her back. But she wasn't sixteen any more, and it was practically impossible to launch someone who had already been 'promising'.

As for Roger Duchesne, he had been a big star before the war. After that he had drifted into the underworld, and been forced by the *milieu* to leave Paris because of his debts. Since I wanted him for my film, I applied to the *milieu* and they allowed him to reappear. I believe he now sells cars near the Porte de Champerret.

People are always talking about my trio of police chiefs (Desailly, Meurisse, Périer) and they will certainly add Bourvil from *Le Cercle Rouge*, but the one who is often forgotten is Guy Decomble in *Bob le Flambeur*. I think he is excellent in the film, a first-rate actor. As a matter of fact, Truffaut used him in *Les Quatre Cents Coups*.

We learn almost nothing about Bob. Is he trying to keep a certain distance between himself and his youth?

We know nothing of Bob's younger days because all he speaks about is his childhood, and he talks about that exactly as Baby Face Martin does when he goes to see his mother – Humphrey Bogart going to see Marjorie Main – in Wyler's *Dead End*.

Bob contemplates the fact of growing old with a certain pleasure instilled by this lucidity, this awareness of his. He is a free man. He has chosen to live in Montmartre because Montmartre, for him, is the only place one *can* live. It's the last refuge. He lives there from night until dawn, in the hour of the wolf. He sleeps only when the sky is completely light.

Bob le Flambeur is a love-letter to Paris, just as my next film, *Deux Hommes dans Manhattan*, was to be a love-letter to New York. And the night is the time for love-letters.

Bob was a letter to a Paris which no longer existed – the Paris of before the war – and it enshrines a nostalgia for the past. Bob is a son of Paris.

Why did you choose to have him live in a painter's studio?

For several reasons. First, there was a studio at 36 Avenue Junot which I would have loved to live in myself, and which I reconstructed as a set (and slept in one night). Second, Roger Duchesne happened to have lived there once. As a matter of fact he was arrested one day at 36 Avenue Junot. And third, I had known a guy there before the war, a man of charm and taste living on the shady side of the law.

During my childhood this was an extraordinarily wild spot. It was called 'the maquis' because where all you can see now is houses there was once real virgin forest. When I was a small boy, I often used to play among the trees, stumps and creepers of the 'maquis de Montmartre' . . . the Paris I knew was still the city of *Les Mystères de Paris*. There were simply fantastic places in some districts.

You must remember that I knew the 'Cité Jeanne d'Arc', and anybody who never knew the 'Cité Jeanne d'Arc' in Paris doesn't know anything. It overlooked the street of the same name, where there are new houses now, quite close to the rue Jenner. It was a 'casbah' where no policeman ever dared set foot and where guys used to hide out when the police were after them. To get into this fabulous Court of Miracles, which was closed to cars because it was so narrow, you had to be with someone who had the open sesame. From time to time the police made raids in an attempt to clean it up, but they just got bottles and things on their heads and had to retreat.

Paris suddenly ceased to be an age-old city of mystery with the arrival of the Germans, although the 'Cité Jeanne d'Arc' itself had disappeared before the war.

Is it because of all these changes that Bob at one point says to the policeman he is lunching with in a Chinese restaurant: 'The milieu isn't the same any more, it's Corruption & Co. now'?

That line was written by Lebreton, based on something I had written earlier, and it demonstrates that there was a great difference between the pre-war and the post-war *milieu*. It is one of the things behind Bob's nostalgia.

The German occupation changed everything. Before the war the *milieu* was one thing and the police another. Then with the occupation you suddenly had the German Gestapo and the French Gestapo, the latter being composed of French policemen and crooks. There were as many police as crooks. The most celebrated Paris Gestapo, the one in the rue Lauriston, included both Abel Danos and Inspector Bony! The *milieu* never recovered from this, but the police just became the police again.

The Gestapo played a curious role in Paris . . . A lot of crooks and writers I knew before the war gave themselves up to it completely. You ought to read a book called *Tu Trahiras sans Vergogne* by Philippe Azzize which is to be published

58

shortly by Fayard and which tells the story of the rue Lauriston. The story isn't quite complete, since there were things that couldn't be told because they concern people who are still alive and in high places even though their conduct during the war was so suspect.

It isn't for nothing that Paul Ricci (Pellegrin) says to Fardiano (Frankeur) in *Le Deuxième Souffle*, 'You swine, you learned your trade in the Gestapo.'

Bob and Roger are bound by ties of friendship. Do you believe in this masculine friendship between crooks?

No, I don't believe in friendship, not masculine friendship between crooks or any other kind. That is one of the things I don't believe in any more, but which I don't know myself and therefore like to have in my films. Rather than friendship, there is community of interest in the *milieu*, and perhaps too a certain inertia . . . when you see each other every afternoon at five for the daily game of cards.

What are the ties between Bob and the Inspector?

All crooks have always had a fellow-feeling for cops, and cops have always had a fellow-feeling for crooks. They're in the same business. They exist in relation to each other.

Bob is a man possessed by gambling fever . . . but you yourself are no gambler. Were you influenced by Sacha Guitry's Roman d'un Tricheur*?*

It's quite possible, because I adore that film. I don't think I was thinking about it while making *Bob le Flambeur*, but it may be that an image or two haunted me. I am thinking of the shot of the man whose face is hidden by the lamp and whom Guitry is about to cheat when he recognizes him as the man who saved his life during the 1914 war . . . Meanwhile, the

59

Bob le Flambeur: Daniel Cauchy and Isabelle Corey

commentary tells us that from that day Guitry stopped cheating.

Why does Bob put a coin in the one-armed bandit he has at home every time he comes in?

Bob is a gambler. This machine gives him a last chance for a flutter before he goes to bed. This is the only kind of gambling I have ever done in my life . . . you know, you put a coin in and try to ring up three lemons or three cherries. I have always wanted to have one of these machines in my room, so I put one in Bob's.

Is there a certain homesickness in Bob? What do Paulo and Anne mean to him?

Paulo is his assistant, whom he eventually comes to look on almost as a son. Like myself with Volker Schlöndorff, you might say . . . more or less. Anne represents the kind of girl who has been around all my life: very young, very high heels, making no distinction between good and evil, and instantly burning their wings under the impression that they are really living. Beautiful girls, who are soon trapped and ground down by the city of men, because of course a city belongs to its men.

In your early films, you used to have scenes of women naked or undressing. But now, when that's just about all one does see on the screen, you have completely eliminated them.

Yes, because it has become a convention. I could do scenes like that when you didn't see them all over the place – always with great tact and discretion. A man and a woman in bed or a girl undressing is almost intolerable now. We are a long way from the famous Hollywood cinema of the thirties, where eroticism existed on a different level. That was a high-class eroticism which flattered the sexual instincts of men and

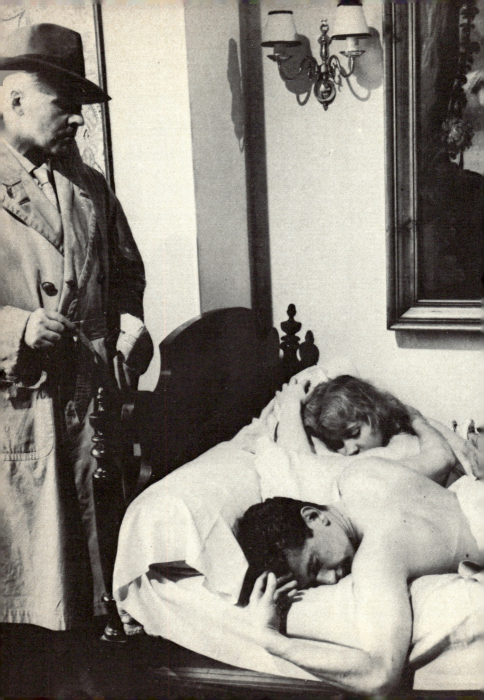

women. There was more eroticism then anyway, when women appeared fully dressed on the screen, than now when they are often completely nude. It has become a sort of vulgar, unattractive habit which offends me greatly. It's my Old Testament side, I think, my puritanism.

In *Le Cercle Rouge* I didn't write a single part for a woman. I did it quite unconsciously, with no purpose in mind, simply in reaction against everything I have had to see over the last three years at the Commission de Censure. Once again I shall be accused of misogyny, of not liking women . . . which is entirely incorrect, I assure you. As I have already told you, in my films I like to show things that I don't know. And unlike certain of my colleagues who are totally obsessed with eroticism, I do know my way around the subject.

But you did show a couple in bed in Bob le Flambeur*?*

Yes, but you must admit that they are asleep. In any case the scene is relevant to the film. Bob, this man of fifty who is in love with a ravishing young girl of sixteen – but who naturally will never tell her – suddenly finds her in his own bed with the boy he loves as a son. In spite of everything he steals away on tiptoe so as not to waken them. All men are a little masochistic, and I rather suspect Bob of having created the situation which lets Paulo and Anne sleep together . . . just to be a little unhappy!

Isn't there an analogy between the Isabelle Corey of Bob le Flambeur *and the Marilyn Monroe of* The Asphalt Jungle*?*

Not exactly, in the sense that Bob is certainly not the sort of man who would let himself be exploited, whereas Louis Calhern is. Bob, let's say, doesn't give money to Anne in the way Calhern does to Marilyn. Bob is more paternal. Alonzo Emmerich (Calhern) undoubtedly has this masochistic need to be victimized by women, and he never gets angry with

63

Bob le Flambeur: 'All men are a little masochistic' (Roger Duchesne, Isabelle Corey, Daniel Cauchy)

Marilyn, even when she double-crosses him, as though he expected to be betrayed. But if you want to talk about Huston's film, we'll be here for the rest of the night. I find it much easier to talk about other people's films than my own . . . Don't forget that I am still – above all – a spectator, and being a spectator is the finest profession in the world.

Would you like to have Bob le Flambeur *reissued?*

No, I don't want to reissue any of my early films. I don't see the point unless it's a financial one, and that doesn't interest me. On the other hand, if I ever find my real script for *Bob le Flambeur* I shall remake it – in colour. But I won't include the hold-up at the Casino, although of course it was quite original. So many people have used it since . . . it's incredible.

Did Bob le Flambeur *cost very much to make?*

Bob cost seventeen and a half million francs, whereas the average film at that time cost a hundred and eighty million. It was a very profitable film for me, because it did very well . . .
   I often say – which isn't true – that I have always been rejected by the profession. Actually, it is I who have always rejected the profession. I have always had offers to make films which I have always refused. I have never been forced into unemployment. I was impossible to deal with, there's no doubt about that, and quarrelled with all the producers.

Why does Bob forget the time of the hold-up?

Simply because, in spite of himself, he is possessed by the gambling demon. You know, there is a shot of Bob in his dinner-jacket at the Deauville Casino, looking down the staircase at the gambling-rooms below, in which he looks exactly like Bela Lugosi. Suddenly, you have Dracula in the film.

64

7 : Deux Hommes dans Manhattan

There was a three-year interval between Bob le Flambeur *and* Deux Hommes dans Manhattan. *What were you doing all this time?*

In the summer of 1957, I began shooting another film which I never completed. At the time I had rented the rue Jenner studios to Pathé-Marconi for three years, so I decided to shoot on location. With this in mind, I had conceived a very cheap, low budget film. Decaë was my cameraman, his wife was his assistant, Pierre Grasset and Dédé Salgues (André Garret) the actors.

This film, which was based on a script I had just finished, was a spy story – the genre hadn't become fashionable yet. Pierre Grasset played the role of a private detective. One evening, after a routine day of shadowing a married woman and her lover, he found an old gentleman waiting in his office who had formerly been his superior officer in the army, and who sought his aid in a very dangerous mission: 'No one in my organization can undertake this mission, because the Atlantic Alliance stipulates, among other things, that there shall never be a counter-espionage service within the Allied espionage services. Officially, we do not have the right to spy on each other . . . I need you to steal some top secret documents from the Americans.'

I shot only one sequence for the film, set almost entirely in the Gare Saint-Lazare. A man with a little attaché-case left the boat-train which had just arrived from Cherbourg. He walked along the platforms, went through the booking-hall, came down the stairs till he arrived at the left-luggage office and checked in the case.

From that moment, Grasset began to follow him. The man walked towards the exit, put the baggage-ticket into an envelope he had ready in his pocket, and dropped it into a post-box for *pneumatiques*. He then retraced his steps and got back on the boat-train which was leaving for Cherbourg. Disconcerted, Grasset didn't know what to do next, since he couldn't get the case without first getting hold of the envelope containing the ticket. So, the only certainty being that the ticket would reach its destination in an hour and a half, he mounted guard beside the left-luggage office.

Meanwhile, the man who had got back on the train jumped off as it slowed down while going through the Gare des Batignolles, crossed the line to emerge on the rue Jouffroy, and calmly hailed a taxi . . . So much for the sequence. As for the film, at a certain point Grasset went to seek assistance from a retired cop, a bit of a drunk and a bit of a bum, who lived with his twenty cats and a gramophone in a corner of Menilmontant which no longer exists now. Which meant that the film was a spy story with two characters who weren't spies.

But to tell you the whole film would take me an hour and a half, the exact running time of the film. In the end, after many adventures, the old cop and Grasset both died. Grasset expired in a telephone booth uttering the words 'Mission Accomplished', which could have served as a title for the film.

Why did you abandon the film?

Because I wasn't a very easy person at the time. I was pretty temperamental . . . it was over a silly argument about the brim of a hat Grasset was to wear. I threw the whole thing up on an impulse.

66

Are there any other films you began and never finished?

Before making *Deux Hommes dans Manhattan*, I had begun writing a thriller which was set in Cannes during the film festival. I had already built the sets and was ready to start when I decided to abandon it because I had once again made the mistake of having a collaborator on the script.

So I abandoned this project and, still with Decaë as my cameraman, began shooting another script called *L'A.F.P. Nous Communique*[1] which I had written quite some time previously. It was a story about a President of the French Cabinet who died of a coronary in his girl-friend's flat. I already had twenty minutes in the can when de Gaulle came to power in May 1958. That was the end of it for me. *L'A.F.P. Nous Communique* died with the Fourth Republic.

And then one day in the summer of 1958, I went with Grasset to the Celtic in the rue d'Arras to see *The Asphalt Jungle* for the *n*th time. In the middle, Grasset suddenly exclaimed, 'Look! Your set!' It was true: the lamp, the divan, the big window, the metal Venetian blinds, everything was there . . . Quite unconsciously I had reconstructed the living-room of Louis Calhern's secret hideaway for my film. We were coming out of the cinema telling ourselves once again that *The Asphalt Jungle* was undoubtedly the greatest film in the world when Grasset said: 'Doesn't that make you want to go on with your film? Doesn't the fact that you un-consciously created a set corresponding exactly to a set in an American film make you want to transpose your story to America?' And that is how I came to transpose the story of *L'A.F.P. Nous Communique* to New York, where I went in November 1958 to shoot the exteriors. The interiors were filmed at the Billancourt Studios the following year, starting in February 1959.

But for Deux Hommes dans Manhattan *you no longer had Decaë?*

1. L'A.F.P. = L'Agence France-Presse.

No, because Decaë wasn't free. He had become cameraman-in-chief to the Nouvelle Vague. Mike Shrayer did the New York scenes in which I appear; all the other shots I did myself. In Paris, Nicolas Hayer took over the interiors, and Charles Bitsch the exteriors.

You once said that the American ideal woman is 'a female with a pair of buttocks in her brassière'. Why do you think they go for that?

I remember that I was very struck in 1958–1959 by the fact that all erotic advertising invariably featured women with unbelievably huge breasts. In the specialized shops in Times Square, all the objects on sale were in the shape of incredible breasts. It really was fantastic. I went with Grasset to several strip-tease joints, where all the strippers were monstrous. And I do mean monstrous; suffering from a physical deformity – because atrophy and hypertrophy *are* diseases – which they must certainly cultivate to please their clients. And this seems to be the American ideal of beauty. You had the feeling that the Americans were suffering from a sort of mammary complex and still needed to be breast-fed. It was very disagreeable, even rather repellent . . .

Wasn't Deux Hommes dans Manhattan *originally to be the portrait of a dead man as seen through the eyes of four different women, rather like the Paul Morand story in* L'Europe Galante?

Yes, there's the Paul Morand story, but there are also two English films: Anthony Asquith's *The Woman in Question* and Basil Dearden's *Sapphire*. But it was the Asquith film in particular, where a murdered woman is described through the men who knew her, that made me change my script.

Why did you choose to have two journalists, rather than police-men, conduct the investigation?

Because at the time I wrote the script, in 1949–1950 that is, I used to spend my evenings at Saint-Germain-des-Prés with two good friends, both journalists: François Nadeau and Jean-François Devay. We were often joined by Georges Dudognon, a photographer, on whom I based the character of Delmas. He was the best news photographer in Paris. The four of us often used to drive around in a car . . . Georges had a Mercedes convertible like the one at the end of *L'Armée des Ombres*. And in my original script, *L'A.F.P. Nous Communique*, the story was set in Paris in a Mercedes convertible . . .

Do you see Deux Hommes dans Manhattan *as a sort of documentary on the world of journalism?*

No, no. You're way off track with questions like that. I never work in realism, and I don't want to. *Deux Hommes dans Manhattan* is not a portrait of the world of journalism because I am not a documentarist. And since I am careful never to be realistic, there is no more inaccurate portraitist than I am. What I do is false. Always.

Pierre Grasset is excellent as Delmas. Did you get on well with him?

Very. I'm extremely fond of Pierre Grasset. He could have had a great career. Belmondo told me that when he saw *Deux Hommes dans Manhattan* he came out of the Marignan very downcast because he thought that this wouldn't be the year of Belmondo but of Grasset. The only trouble was that my film didn't take a penny. To carve out a career for himself Grasset would have had to accept living without money. You have to go through that to be an actor. If I were to ask him tomorrow to play a part in a film, he would come at once, but he would never ask anything of anybody. In this business you have to push, and he doesn't give a damn. He always waits for offers to come in, and that's why he doesn't work more often. He's a good actor, handsome and with a lot of presence. It's a shame the industry doesn't use him more often.

Grasset is a strange character. You could almost make a film about him. I remember you could see him every afternoon sitting on the terrace of the Belle Ferronière with the air of somebody who has never done a hand's turn in his life. Very *vitellone*. Actually, he was a commercial traveller and used to get up every morning at 3 a.m. to catch the train to visit his out-of-town clients, and be back by the afternoon.

Deux Hommes dans Manhattan wasn't successful because the time wasn't ripe for a film like that . . . this was before the Nouvelle Vague . . . and because it was shown in a big cinema, the Marignan – there weren't any small ones yet. Don't forget that it was the Marignan that killed Jacques Becker's *Le Trou*.

I remember when my film came out, Jacques said: 'I'm going to flop, too, because I'm getting the same cinema as you.' I told him he was crazy and that *Le Trou* was a very different proposition from *Deux Hommes dans Manhattan*, but it made no difference. After listening to me, he simply said, 'You'll see.' Well, it was true, I did see. He didn't see it because he died before then, but I did . . .

Why did you play the part of Moreau?

God only knows! Through some irreparable idiocy, especially as it wasn't at all a role for me. I am not a character actor . . . At first I thought I was going to play a small part to get myself out of a spot in New York, and then all of a sudden I found myself completely trapped. I don't think it matters, however, because I think it's an unimportant film.

Moreau seems to be the hero of the film, and Delmas the villain . . .

Only seems. The whole film is built on this seems. Actually, it's Moreau who is the contemptible one. Delmas is a man

Deux Hommes dans Manhattan: 'A shabby, pedantic little clerk' (Melville as Moreau)

who is good at his job, a real professional. Moreau is just an employee, a shabby, pedantic little clerk.

This is made clear at the beginning of the film: when he is summoned, Moreau only goes after tidying up his desk.

Exactly. But nobody understood because I was playing the role. I could at a pinch have played Delmas, but I was too old for the character. It was a bad mistake, because I was physically wrong for Moreau. Total miscasting.

We see Moreau full face only when he arrives in Aubert's office (Jean Lara). Why not right away?

So that I shouldn't be recognized immediately. I wanted to draw attention solely to my movements, to the clerkish aspect of the character.

The sequence in the hospital, where Delmas forces the secret out of Fèvre-Berthier's mistress, caused you to be accused of gratuitous violence. But this method of getting information or photographs is quite common.

It's a little rough, I admit, but you have to shake people up in their seats a bit. The viciousness of Delmas's behaviour towards the poor girl who has tried to kill herself . . . my God, we've seen it often enough. Do you remember the business of the photographs of Piaf in Casablanca weeping for the death of Cerdan with his wife Marinette?

Had I been a news photographer, I would have always been after the document and I would probably have behaved very badly. I know a news photographer who spent the night in a cupboard in the room where Gréco and Lemaire spent their wedding-night. In the end he didn't dare take a single photograph and ran away through the garden to the rue de Berry with Lemaire on his heels. In this business, where does the point begin beyond which you must not go? I sincerely believe that there are no limits.

A news photographer is a hunter. A hunter of pictures. Anything goes in flushing the game. If he really loves his job, his fingers should be itching to press the shutter, otherwise he ought just to change jobs.

Why does Delmas finally renounce the opportunity to earn so much money by throwing the roll of film into the gutter?

Because in his alcoholic, after Moreau hits him, he suddenly sees the eyes of Fèvre-Berthier's girl. The only thing which could bring a man like Delmas to this point of renunciation is a woman's eyes. And not necessarily because he is a photographer. Mr Bernstein (Everett Sloane) in *Citizen Kane* isn't a photographer, and yet he thinks every day of a woman's face which he merely glimpsed on a passing ferry-boat as he crossed the Hudson. 'A white dress she had on, and she was

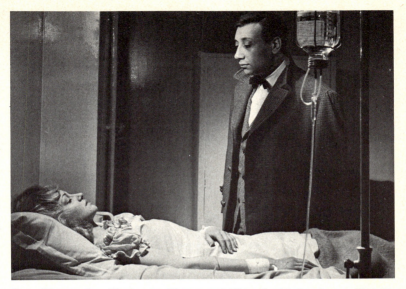

Deux Hommes dans Manhattan: Moreau and Fèvre-Berthier's mistress (Melville and Ginger Hall)

carrying a white parasol . . . and I only saw her for one second and she didn't see me at all.' And it's true: the face of a woman barely glimpsed, or her eyes, can haunt you for years. It has happened to me . . .

Where did you get the ideas for the apartment belonging to the two Lesbians?

That apartment is an exact reconstruction, without any invention, of a homosexual's apartment I had seen in Greenwich Village at the time.

When McKimmie (Jerry Mengo) talks to him about the 'roaring twenties', Moreau tells him: 'You're nostalgic for the twenties.'

73

It was something between Jerry and me, rather than dialogue for the film, because he had spent his childhood in New York. He told me, for instance, that in the mid twenties every carriage in the Third Avenue subway had a coal stove . . . he had marvellous memories which suggested the end of the nineteenth century rather than 1925.

There are very few camera movements in the film. You use pans, but only one tracking shot – to discover the singer during the recording session.

In the course of a single day I had seen two films without tracking shots, Elia Kazan's *A Face in the Crowd* and John Ford's *How Green Was My Valley* (actually there was a forty-centimetre track for reframing in the Ford, and a track in to Walter Matthau in the Kazan), and I wanted to try it myself. Just to see.

Visually, the film is rather dark, without much light. Is New York like that?

Yes, absolutely. Except for Times Square, I assure you that in 1958 New York was a dark city. Much more so than Paris. I remember that from the window of my room on the ninth floor, looking out over 85th Street, I couldn't see what was going on below. I could hear cars passing and see their head-lights, but I couldn't see the street. New York is as dark as it is beautiful.

How do you rate Deux Hommes dans Manhattan *in your work nowadays?*

I don't. I reject it. Rejection of your own films is a very healthy, hygienic attitude. It prevents you from taking your-self seriously, and taking yourself seriously is tragic. How do you reject a film? By making another. It's the only way.

Deux Hommes dans Manhattan: Christiane Eudès and Melville

At one moment in *Deux Hommes dans Manhattan* you see a packet of Boyard cigarettes on a bed. I did that shot for Godard. It was his brand, the only one he smoked. That was when I liked Godard. Since then . . .

8 : Léon Morin, Prêtre

In 1959, you played the role of a novelist in Jean-Luc Godard's first feature, A Bout de Souffle.

I agreed to play Parvulesco to please Godard. He had written to me asking me to appear in the film: 'Try to talk about women just as you do normally.' Which is what I did. I had seen Nabokov in a televised interview, and being, like him, subtle, pretentious, pedantic, a bit cynical, naïve, etc., I based the character on him. My sequence ran for over ten minutes, and *A Bout de Souffle* for more than three hours! It had to be cut down to a normal running time, and Godard asked my advice. I told him to cut everything which didn't keep the action moving, and to remove all unnecessary scenes, mine included. He didn't listen to me, and instead of cutting whole scenes as was the practice then, he had the brilliant idea of cutting more or less at random within scenes. The result was excellent.

Godard refers to *Bob le Flambeur* in *A Bout de Souffle*, in the scene where Belmondo-Poiccard tries to get a friend in the Inter-Americana travel agency to cash a cheque. When he is refused, he says, 'Your friend Bob Montagné would cash it for me,' to which the other guy replies, 'He's in jail, poor sod.'

What do you think of the Nouvelle Vague style?

There's no such thing. The Nouvelle Vague was an inexpensive way of making films. That's all.

I asked you this question because Henri Decoin told me shortly before his death that his best film was Tendre et Violente Elisabeth, *which was beset by innumerable financial problems. He felt that because of these difficulties, which often forced him to exercise his imagination and ingenuity, he had achieved something like a Nouvelle Vague style.*

Decoin wasn't telling you the truth. It's distressing: he was a good friend and he is dead now . . .

Claude Durand, who worked with Decoin on that film, was my editor for a long time. One day around six o'clock in the afternoon she saw him rush into the cutting-rooms like a madman, shouting: 'Take out all the pencil-marks, take out everything, everything . . . I don't want fades, dissolves, or anything . . . I've just seen *A Bout de Souffle.*'

In spite of your taste for the classical and your obsession with perfection, you seem to see your films as rough drafts. Why is this?

Because it is only after a film is finished and ready for release that one sees the immense number of things one might have done but didn't. It's then that one wants to begin all over again . . . as Jacques Becker did with *Le Trou.* Not content with the draft that every film has to be, Jacques Becker entirely re-shot *Le Trou* . . . in my rue Jenner studios. He did twenty, twenty-five, twenty-eight, thirty, thirty-three takes of every scene, invariably using the first, second, third, or at most, sixth. It was perfection in reverse. I remember that even after his twentieth take he'd still feel the need to turn to his son Jean and see him nod 'Yes'. He seemed to be paying attention to what Jean thought. It was incredible!

Each time you mention Le Trou, *it is clear that this film has a special place in your heart.*

Not only because of the film, which I think is one of the greatest in the world, but because of Jacques.

Becker was the only French film-maker to bother himself about me when I was on my own. One day in 1948 I received a telephone call: 'Hallo, Becker here. This morning Jean Renoir and I saw *Le Silence de la Mer*, and I'd like to meet you for a drink.' I was a shy young man and found it difficult to ask him what he'd thought of my film. He'd loved it, and won me over completely by talking to me as though I were an old friend. When I asked him, still rather timidly, what Renoir's reaction had been after the screening, he replied: 'Well, Jean said something that wasn't very nice from my point of view. He said that *Le Silence de la Mer* was the best film he'd seen for fifteen years. And as I've made quite a few since showing him my first . . .' Wonderful Becker!

To show you what an important role Becker played in my life, I'll tell you a little story. One day I was sitting with my wife in the café Dupont-Ternes, opposite the Cinéac-Ternes where *Les Enfants Terribles* had just opened. All I had in my pocket was thirty-five francs: thirty francs for the Coca-Cola, and five for a tip. This was twenty years ago, in the spring of 1950. For various reasons I had definitely decided to give up film-making. I really couldn't go on. The previous evening, sitting on a bench in the Avenue Montaigne, I had spoken about this to an old friend I was very fond of, Pière Colombier, brother of the art director, who was once a film-maker but had now turned tramp. This old man, who had once been a king of Paris but was now wretched and penniless, still had the fire to revive my spirits: 'You have no right to do that. It's a hard profession, I agree, but it's the finest in the world. Believe me!' And the better to convince me, he talked about the days when he was making films: *Le Roi des Resquilleurs*, *Les Rois du Sport*, etc. His words revived me, but not enough to sway me from my decision to abandon it all. So there I was in the café by the Cinéac-Ternes when, just as we were leaving, Jacques Becker and Daniel Gélin came out from inside. 'It's incredible,'

Becker said when he saw us, 'we've been sitting inside for two hours talking about *Les Enfants Terribles* which we've just seen again. It's a marvellous film.' I couldn't even ask them to have a drink, but after they had left and we had climbed into our dilapidated old car, my wife and I were serene and happy. It was a sign, you see . . . and I didn't give up the cinema.

Jacques Becker died of haemochromatosis. The organs of his body fabricated iron which it could not eliminate. When he died, he was transformed into a statue of iron. He was handsome, so handsome on his death-bed, Jacques Becker. Those who saw him will never forget.

I saw *Le Trou* one morning at the Marignan. Jean Becker and the manager of the cinema were up in the balcony. My wife and I were in the stalls, just the two of us in that immense auditorium. Jean knew that I was a friend of his father. When I got home after seeing that masterpiece, I went to bed, just overwhelmed.

How did you come to make Léon Morin, Prêtre?

The failure of *Deux Hommes dans Manhattan* didn't cause me any problems. My career wasn't at stake and it wasn't a breakdown. On the contrary: I owned my own studios, and was more or less immune. But I had no intention of going on making unsuccessful films. I had had enough of being an *auteur maudit* known only to a handful of crazy film-buffs.

Early in 1960 I was busy with the production of an expensive short film, Jean Wagner's *Ce Monde Banal*, which was a story about a French soldier and a German girl set in occupied Germany. I advised him to transpose the action to Algeria, which was very much in the news at that time. Wagner liked the suggestion, and after transforming his soldier into a 'para' and the German girl into an Algerian, shot the film in three days at my Jenner studios in very handsome sets built for the occasion. Henri Decaë, whom I had bought back specially from the Hakim Brothers for twice what he was worth, was the cameraman, and Philippe Leroy and Nadia Lara the actors. It really was big budget stuff. But Wagner was unable to edit and mix his film, which he had done in seventy-five shots – actually it would have been fascinating done in a single take. That's when I realized what a terribly dangerous business producing can be. But I must say that if this first effort had succeeded, I would certainly have gone on to produce more films by other people.

After this, in September 1960, I bought the rights to an American thriller which I wanted to film and which I proposed to the most powerful French producer-distributor, Edmond Tenoudji. He told me exactly what Ray Ventura had told me once before, and suggested that I should become a 'jobbing' producer for him, using as director a young man who was very much in vogue that September but isn't any longer. But I couldn't set it up, and as Georges de Beauregard and Carlo Ponti wanted me to make a film for them, I finally decided to adapt *Léon Morin, Prêtre*.

Does Béatrix Beck's novel correspond to the war as you knew it?

It corresponds to much of my experience, not necessarily to my war . . . France under the Occupation, for instance. But what attracted me to this book, which I had wanted to film ever since it was published in November 1952, was the character of Léon Morin – because I believe that this non-autobiographical way of revealing oneself is peculiar to all creators, and had I been a priest I would have acted as he did.

I think I reveal myself enormously through my films. In each of his ventures a film-maker must be able to disguise himself in a costume tailored to his material. I often say that if I were making a film about black Africa, I'd become a black African while shooting the film; if I were making a film about the Indian minorities of North America, I'd become a Sioux or an Apache during shooting; in a film about homosexuals, I would be a homosexual, and so on. Do you see what I mean?

Léon Morin, Prêtre

I would think exactly like the character I was dealing with.

*This is the first of three films you made in a row with Belmondo.
How did you meet him?*

The very first time I met Jean-Paul Belmondo was in the
scene in *A Bout de Souffle* where he is coming down the stairs
at Orly, facing the camera, and I am going up the same stairs
with my back to the camera. All we did was pass each other.
He had just finished his part, and I was just beginning mine.
   My first real meeting with him was in Italy while he was
making *La Ciociara (Two Women)* with Sophia Loren under
the direction of Vittorio De Sica. Carlo Ponti had invited me
to spend the week-end with him so that I could talk to
Belmondo about my intention of using him in *Léon Morin,
Prêtre*. Belmondo was very reticent about the project, not to

say completely hostile, simply because he was afraid.

We met on the locations where *La Ciociara* was being shot, between Naples and Rome, in a spot where I had served during the war. But the astonishing thing was that the film he was making told a story about us, about French soldiers, but represented as Moroccan troops in De Sica's film. Actually the men who committed those rapes in Italy were not Moroccans, who would have been incapable of such acts, but French soldiers. It had quite an effect on me, suddenly finding myself back there . . .

And why did you choose Emmanuelle Riva to play Barny?

No one but she could play Béatrix Beck. I knew Béatrix Beck, so I had to find someone who resembled her, who was like her, and . . . I must say I'm very happy with my choice. I don't see who else I could have used instead.

I had seen Emmanuelle Riva in *Hiroshima mon Amour* and liked her very much. She isn't at all easy to direct because she's terribly nervous, but she is a great actress. I think she's fantastic in *Léon Morin, Prêtre*.

What about the rest of the cast – how did you choose them?

I chose Irène Tunc because she incarnated the mental image I had of Christine Sangredin, she had the Lyonnais accent, she was beautiful . . .

There are four Gozzi sisters in *Léon Morin, Prêtre*. In one amusing shot the character of France is played simultaneously by two of them. It's a trick shot: as Marielle turned her head to the left, I replaced her with Patricia, who then completed the movement begun by her younger sister. So in one shot I show the baby grown into a little girl; but people don't notice because it is Marielle's voice in both halves of the sentence spoken by France over the shot. There are always a lot of things in my films which are designed not to be noticed.

82

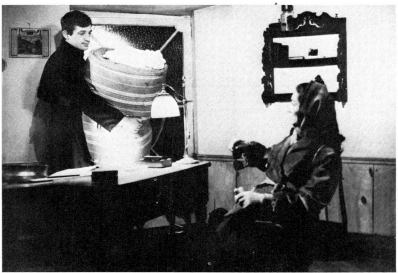

Léon Morin, Prêtre: Belmondo with Monique Bertho (*above*) and Emmanuelle Riva

As for Monique Hennessy, who plays the part of Arlette, she was my secretary and I had already used her in *Deux Hommes dans Manhattan*, where she plays the prostitute who says, 'So kind of you to visit me. Tell me, pretty boys, are you in a hurry or not?' I used her again in *Le Doulos*, where she is murdered by Belmondo. Monique might have gone places . . . I have known so many girls who might have gone places!

What was the main idea in Léon Morin, Prêtre? *The impossibility of conversion?*

No, that was only one element. Conversion doesn't take up a man's whole life, only a moment in it. The main idea was to show this amorous priest who likes to excite girls but doesn't sleep with them. Léon Morin is Don Juan; he has the women all crazy about him. Well aware of his physical attraction and his intelligence, he makes maximum use of these assets.

Are you also denouncing mysticism as an imposture?

Ah, no, I don't want to talk about things like that. Personally I have no idea whether mysticism is an imposture. Everyone has the right to be what he is and to believe what he likes. In any case I don't think that *Léon Morin, Prêtre* is an anti-religious film or that it can be taken as such. On the contrary, I believe it is a very Catholic film. So did the French Catholic Church, since it adopted the film after it was finished. Before, the Church was very, very prudent, even a little 'anti', because it gave me no help during shooting . . .

You know, I believe that personal opinions have nothing to do with cinematographic problems . . . What I think of faith, of the non-existence of God, of Socialism and so on, is my private world, a world which I try not to put into my films because I don't think it's my business to offer messages – political, metaphysical or whatever . . . It may be the business of other film-makers to discuss the big questions; personally, though I don't mind touching on them, I have no wish to explore them.

But you aren't a religious person, are you?

No, definitely not.

Then what do you understand by religion and faith?

I'll answer that from a personal point of view, nothing to do with the film. I think that religion is useful if one considers it as a moral foundation. As a matter of fact, it *has* been useful . . . because there was a religious morality before there were civic or lay moralities. Faith is something that eludes me because I can't conceive of believing in something that doesn't exist. I don't understand how people can believe in God any more than in Father Christmas. Why do people tell children that Father Christmas doesn't exist, and never tell adults that God doesn't exist? They seem to let this other legendary character go on for ever. To me they are two brothers, God and Father Christmas. They exist only in the minds of children and child-adults. Nevertheless, I do know some very intelligent men who believe in God, so I really can't go so far as to say that people who believe in God are fools. All the same it's amazing. It's quite beyond me.

For me faith, whether in God or Marx, is a thing of the past.

Is Barny's conversion in Léon Morin, Prêtre *a false conversion?*

Of course. She becomes converted in order to get laid. But she isn't aware of this. She really believes in her conversion. She has come close to the priest, to his thoughts, but suddenly this isn't enough; she must make love with the agent of God.

Do you see Morin as a militant priest without frustrations?

Come now! A priest is always frustrated. Look at how the only people asking to be allowed to marry at the moment are the priests. No one wants to get married any more except them. In any case Léon Morin is a man, and men need to make themselves suffer . . . being a priest is a way of making oneself suffer.

Is it true that Léon Morin, Prêtre *originally ran for over three hours?*

Yes, it ran for three hours and thirteen minutes, and I cut it down to two hours eight. Both distributor and producers were very pleased with the film in the full version, and even tried to prevent me from cutting it. I had to appeal to Carlo Ponti, and he gave me a free hand because I was the author of the film. I had created a sort of great fresco of the Occupation, of the obsession with food, of all the things, including sex, that obsess a woman on her own. Then suddenly the only aspect that continued to interest me was this story of an unfulfilled love-affair between Léon Morin and Barny. Originally, Léon Morin made his appearance only after an hour and a quarter; in the final version he appears after a quarter of an hour. Nevertheless, the film was good, and I wonder now whether I was maybe wrong to cut it . . . or maybe I was right, I don't know.

I cut an excellent scene in which Barny begged Léon Morin to let her warn the young girl accused of fraternizing with the Germans, Gilberte Lathuile, that she was going to be shot by the Maquisards. It was extraordinary because of the priest's attitude, and Jean-Paul was first rate in it. The trouble was it was dependent on the stuff I had cut . . .

What about the scene in the book where Barny finds Lucienne crying over an open book, and realizes that it is a cookery book and not a novel which has moved her to tears?

I did shoot that . . . it was a marvellous scene. It's a wonderful

86

book! I often re-read it you know. On the other hand, I didn't shoot the scene where Christine describes the terrible death of a child who is killed by an Italian soldier. I like Italians, and I didn't want to show them in an unsympathetic light.

Did you shoot other scenes which you didn't retain in the final cut?

I didn't keep the scenes dealing with the Maquis and their activities; the scenes with Anton and Minna Silmann; or the sequence where Barny and Christine are playing at bullfights and where Irène Tunc took off her blouse and had nothing on underneath.

A scene I didn't shoot was the one in which Barny, in trousers, tries to seduce Léon Morin in his soutane. I didn't want to spoil the vertical pan in *L'Armée des Ombres* which shows a girl in trousers kissing a Scottish soldier in a kilt. I had to choose . . .

The relationships between the female characters are rather equivocal.

They're not equivocal, they're very clear. I love the way Barny describes Sabine Lévy, with whom she is in love: 'She's like an Amazon . . . Pallas . . . a Samurai.'

You had several editors on the film, among them Nadine Marquand, who has since become a director . . .

Yes: Denise de Casabianca, Nadine Marquand, Jacqueline Meppiel, Marie-Josephe Yoyotte and Agnès Guillemot. I didn't list them all on the credits because Casabianca and Guillemot worked very little on the film. But I listed the other three in order of preference. They then all banded together to sue Georges de Beauregard. I went along to plead my own case and obtained a decision from the court which is now law in France, whereby it is the director who establishes the

Léon Morin, Prêtre: 'She's like an Amazon . . .' (Emmanuelle Riva and Nicole Mirel)

credits. And the title-card on which they were listed in order of preference remained in the film.

Do you know how I met Marie-Josephe Yoyotte? One day Cocteau telephoned me to say, 'I'm sending you a girl called Marie-Josephe Yoyotte. I think she could play Dargélos in *Les Enfants Terribles*.' As soon as I had met her I phoned Cocteau to ask, 'Are you crazy?' 'Yes,' he said, 'maybe!'

9: Le Doulos

Volker Schlöndorff, who is now a director himself, was your assistant on Léon Morin, Prêtre *and* Le Doulos. *You seem to think very highly of him?*

I met Volker one evening at the Ciné-Club du Lycée Montaigne. Bertrand Tavernier had dragged me there to see that monstrosity called *Johnny Guitar*. After the screening, I remember, the session was chaired by a 'priest' who harangued, insulted, thundered, fulminated from his pulpit. This extraordinary character, who turned out a boy who didn't share his opinion of the film and who wore a huge cross on his jacket, was Henri Agel. Ah, tolerance!

Beside Tavernier there was a small boy to whom I paid no attention: Volker Schlöndorff. That was in the spring of 1960. In the summer of the same year, this boy telephoned me to ask if he could become my assistant. I had him come to my office in the rue Jenner. We got on at once. Almost immediately I felt that I had met my spiritual son, and I still feel the same way about him today.

Volker also assisted me in preparing *L'Ainé des Ferchaux* and *Trois Chambres dans Manhattan*. One day while we were working on one or other of these films, he tried to convince me that Eastman Colour was far superior to Technicolor. To prove that he was wrong, I took him to see Lubitsch's *Heaven*

Can Wait, in which Don Ameche played the part of Mr Van Cleve. I don't need to tell you that Volker was dazzled by the film and never again spoke ill of Technicolor.

At the time, I was living in the Hôtel Raphael on the Avenue Kléber. The following day, just as we were going to have dinner after a long day's work, we saw a man in a pelisse and a black homburg in the corridor of the Raphael. I turned to Volker and whispered, 'Look! Just like Mr Van Cleve.' Being something of a joker, I went up to the man and said, 'How do you do, Mr Van Cleve?' He turned round . . . and it was Don Ameche! I couldn't think what to say – the apparition seemed like magic.

Nothing quite so extraordinary had happened to me since 1938, when I was doing my military service at Fontainebleau. One day as I was walking down the main street with a friend, I noticed a man in front of us who was out walking with his wife. He was wearing knickerbockers and hose. Looking at his thick neck made me think of Erich von Stroheim. To amuse my comrade, I fell in step with the couple and addressed the man with the words Stroheim spoke to Pierre Fresnay in *La Grande Illusion*: 'De Boeldieu, from man to man, come back!' The man was Stroheim. He shook my hand vigorously, and took a visiting-card from his pocket. On it he wrote, 'From a soldier to a soldier', then gave it to me and embraced me. He behaved exactly like a general awarding a decoration.

One of the great regrets in my life is that I never made a film with Stroheim.

Before making Le Doulos, *you had signed a contract with Georges de Beauregard to make a film called* Les Dons Juan. *What happened?*

Georges was anxious for me to make a film from a Prosper Mérimée story, *Les Ames du Purgatoire*, which he thought was marvellous. It was a rather ordinary story of one of the two Don Juans of Spanish legend, but I agreed. In a situation like that, always tell the producer his idea is brilliant and then think about the changes you can make. So, starting from the Mérimée story, I wrote an original script intended for Jean-Paul Belmondo and Anthony Perkins. This film, which was to have been a libertine film – *not* an erotic one, let's get that straight – never came off because Jean-Paul asked for a fee of fifty million francs and Georges de Beauregard refused to pay him that much. He thought it was immoral to pay so much to someone he had launched.

While trying to find another actor for the part, I had I don't know how many scripts written on the subject: one by Monique Lange, another by Michel Mardore – which was excellent – and a third by France Roche. The copies of all these scripts, mine included, were destroyed in the fire at the rue Jenner.

Then one day de Beauregard arrived at the rue Jenner in a terrible state. He was green and glassy-eyed. 'Jean-Pierre,' he said, 'I'm finished. I'm going bust!' He had already signed all the contracts with Chabrol, Sagan, Rabier, Michèle Morgan, Danielle Darrieux, Charles Denner, etc. to make *Landru*, which was to be produced by United Artists, when United Artists told him they were dropping the film. Without United Artists, it was impossible for him to honour his contracts. To extricate himself from the fix, Georges de Beauregard planned to sell *Landru* in Rome, but in order to get rid of the Chabrol film he needed a 'locomotive'. 'You're going to make *L'Aîné des Ferchaux* with Belmondo next August,' he said, 'but I know he'd be willing to make another film with you immediately. Now don't tell me that in the whole Série Noire there isn't one book you would like to film right now . . .' And in fact there was a book by Pierre Lesou which I particularly liked: *Le Doulos*. I therefore agreed, but on one condition *sine qua non*: that Reggiani play the role of Maurice Faugel.

The day after this conversation, Georges de Beauregard telephoned me from Rome to say that the matter was settled. However Reggiani, who had just read the book, wanted to play Silien. Reggiani's speciality is always to want the part he isn't offered. If someone asked him to play Armand Duval, he'd be quite capable of saying he wanted to play Marguerite Gauthier!

I was determined to have Belmondo as Silien. I thought it would be amusing to have him go from priest to stool-pigeon. I was just considering letting the whole thing drop when Reggiani decided to change his mind.

One funny thing was that it was only when *Le Doulos* was finished and Belmondo saw himself on the screen that he realized, with great astonishment, 'Christ! The stoolie is me!'

You suppressed all the argot *in the book?*

Yes. I can't stand *argot* in the cinema. When I was young and thought it was genuinely romantic, I indulged in it for a long time . . . it became second nature. Gradually, as I grew older, I cut it out, but when Florence first knew me I talked virtually nothing but *argot*. For a long time I kept . . . 'bad company' . . .

How does it happen that you knew the milieu *so well?*

Among other gangs before the war there was the Gare Saint-Lazare gang. Originally this gang was made up of pupils from the Lycée Condorcet who lived in the west and north-west suburbs. In time we left school but continued to hang around Saint-Lazare. I must say that by the end of 1939 we were a real gang of hooligans . . . we were no longer children. We have all become something else now, but in those days we weren't bothered by scruples. We played tough. But that's another story . . .

All the characters in Le Doulos *are much more ambiguous than the characters in the original novel . . .*

Yes, the characters are all *double*, they are all false. I even

92

signal this to the spectator at the beginning of the film with that truncated line from Céline:

'ONE MUST CHOOSE . . .
DIE . . . OR LIE?'

I cut the end, which is 'ME, I LIVE!'

Le Doulos is a very complicated film, very difficult to understand, because I gave a double twist to the situations in the novel.

Was Lesou happy with the changes you made?

Yes. He even said I should have told him my story before he wrote the book. There's another thriller by Lesou I would have liked to adapt – *Main Pleine* – it's ten times better than *Le Doulos*. But it was filmed by Michel Deville in 1964 under the title *Lucky Jo*. He made a complete mess of it. It makes me sick when I think of it. If you knew the film that could have been made . . . !

It's obvious you have a certain affection for the character of Nuttheccio in Le Doulos?

In the average French film, the role of Nuttheccio would have been played by Dario Moreno, wouldn't it? Well, I wanted a villain who wouldn't cringe in a cold sweat the moment he realizes he's going to die.

I didn't want Dario Moreno, or Dalio, or Claude Cerval, anyone like that. When I telephoned Piccoli to ask if he would help me out by doing a spot in my film, he immediately said yes without waiting for details. He did the part without even reading the script or knowing how much he was going to be paid. I told him that this spot would do him a lot of good, and he simply said 'I know!' He is excellent in the film.

But Nuttheccio isn't closer to me than the other characters. I would certainly face death like him, but I would behave like Silien if I were a police informer. On the other hand, if I were a man embittered by prison and eager to avenge the death of my wife, I would behave like Faugel. And if I were a police superintendent, I would behave exactly like Clain. I always escape through my characters. Making films means being all the actors at once, living other lives . . .

Are you happy with Desailly, your second police superintendent?

Yes, I think he's magnificent. I wanted Clain to be of middle-class background and to have, in addition to the vices and virtues of his class, that layer of cynicism and vulgarity which all policemen acquire after associating with crooks for a certain number of years. I must say that Desailly's interpretation of the character was perfect.

In general, I think my gallery of policemen is quite successful, and corresponds to a certain truth, even though I take care never to be realistic.

You obtain a quality of underplaying from your actors which is particularly evident in Le Doulos.

It was an American actor – of course – who invented under-playing: Fred MacMurray. The uncharitable say that this came about because he couldn't act, but it isn't true. Even today, when you see Fred MacMurray's early films, you can't help being astonished by the economy of means with which he achieves his effects. Looking at the films of that period, one can see that it was only after he had shown the way that other actors – Bogart, for instance – tuned to the same pitch. In the American cinema today, James Garner might be considered the great champion of underplaying.

But he's very bad in Wyler's The Loudest Whisper.

Nothing's bad in that film. It's a masterpiece. Your lack of taste appals me!

To my mind the masterpiece is the first version of The Loudest Whisper, *which Wyler directed in 1936 under the title of* These Three, *with Joel McCrea in the role played later by Garner.*

You're wrong. Do you think that Wyler would bother to re-make a successful film? It's because he knows he failed the first time that he made the second version. I assure you that to anyone who knows the American upper middle classes of Philadelphia and Boston, *The Loudest Whisper* is a magnificent film.

Somehow, simply through your settings, you manage to cast a sort of spell over Le Doulos.

But for the sixty-three American directors who invented talkies in the thirties, I would never have made *Le Doulos.* The settings in my film attest my passion for a kind of film-making that inspired my vocation.

The telephone booth from which Silien calls Salignari but which isn't a French one; the bar we see Volker Schlöndorff entering and which bears no resemblance to a French café; the sash-windows with slatted metal blinds instead of the usual French shutters – all this helps to cast the spell you mention over the audience, but without alienating it.

The same thing is true of Clain's office where the interrogation takes place. It is an exact copy of the office Rouben Mamoulian had built for *City Streets,* and which he copied from the New York police headquarters.

There was a magnificent scene in *City Streets* where Guy Kibbee, after slipping out to commit a murder, told the cop who came to question him a few minutes after the crime that he hadn't stirred all evening. He was sitting in an armchair with a half-smoked cigar in his hand: the ash was undisturbed on the tip – his girl had been smoking it in his absence. There's a marvellous idea for an alibi which one can't use again. Not everybody can dream up ideas like that: it takes a great artist. I love ideas for alibis, this one in particular.

Le Doulos: The Inspector and the Informer (Jean Desailly, Jean-Paul Belmondo); and (*below*) Belmondo, Reggiani, Aimé de March

Le Doulos: 'A man before a mirror means a stock-taking' (Serge Reggiani, *above*); and Reggiani in a street scene by courtesy of 'the sixty-three American directors'

How did you do that shot in Clain's office which lasts for nine minutes and thirty-eight seconds?

We rehearsed solidly all one Friday. By the end of the day, when everything was ready, I was exhausted, especially as I always feel washed out around 6.30. Georges de Beauregard had noticed this, and wanted me to stop work at this time every day. That's the nice thing about Georges: he was ready to lose a fortune so that I could knock off an hour and a half early every evening.

The next day Henri Tiquet, my operator, recited the dialogue for all the characters to me while rehearsing the camera movements I had given him. Then I called in the actors and we shot it. You can't imagine the technical problems we had to overcome to get that shot.

I did an equally difficult though much briefer shot in Delon's room in *Le Samouraï*. But Delon's room wasn't full of glass like Clain's office. Here in *Le Doulos* we constantly ran the risk of getting our reflections in shot, so that at certain moments the entire technical crew had to hide behind the camera. Except the boom operator. He was the invisible man. Dressed in black from head to toe, with even a black hood on, he didn't create any reflections.

By four o'clock in the afternoon we had a completely successful take in the can: the sixth. Just to be sure, I wanted to duplicate it, but had nothing but false starts and fluffs until the fourteenth take, which was perfect up to the fast pan from Belmondo to Marcel Cuvelier. I then shot a fifteenth to complete this one, starting with the pan and continuing to the end. So fourteen and fifteen made a complete take, linked by the fast pan. Although it was as good as the sixth and no one would have noticed the join because it came over the three fuzzy images of the pan, it was the sixth I used in the final cut. Just as a matter of principle.

As a matter of fact, bringing off a shot like that was pretty extraordinary. I remember that just at the moment when

Clain, Silien and the two cops went out of the door and out of shot, my assistant cameraman announced that there was no more film in the camera. We had been shooting uninterruptedly for nine minutes thirty-eight seconds. A thousand feet, in other words.

In the final sequence, Silien is mortally wounded, yet he still takes time out to look at himself in the mirror before dying. It's a very Melvillian ending.

Yes . . . the man face to face with himself . . . Silien need lie no longer. But the end is not exactly as I had conceived it. Silien's last words, 'Fabienne? . . . I won't be coming tonight,' weren't planned that way. What I wanted, after he got to the telephone, was for him to dial a number, and you would hear, 'Hallo, this is the police. Hallo?' That his last reflex should be an impulse to go and telephone the police made a much better ending. It was only when he heard the voice at the other end that he saw the inanity of his gesture and hung up without saying a word. It was at that moment he realized he was already dead. Unfortunately I shot the other version, as used in the film.

Do you see the thriller as the only way of transposing classical tragedy?

I have no use for the Luchino Visconti type of society drama. Tragedy doesn't go at all well with dinner-jackets and frilly shirtfronts: it has come down in the world. Tragedy is the immediacy of death that you get in the underworld, or at a particular time such as war . . . The characters from *L'Armée des Ombres* are tragic characters; you know it from the very beginning.

Maybe that's why you have been accused of treating the theme of the Resistance exactly as you did the theme of Le Doulos.

99

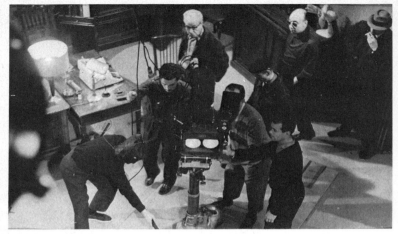

Le Doulos: Filming the nine-minute thirty-eight-second shot in Clain's office (Nicolas Hayer, Melville, Belmondo)

Very probably. I feel no need to apologize.

What about the Western? Isn't that an ideal form for transposing tragedy?

All my original scripts, without exception, are transposed Westerns. But I don't think you can make a Western outside America. That's why I don't like Sergio Leone's films. I've already had offers to make Westerns in Spain . . . but although I'm a 'European' who would love to make Westerns, I shall always refuse to make phoney ones. The really crazy, amazing thing is that the Americans themselves like these Spanish Westerns. They prefer *Once Upon a Time in the West* to the real thing. At the moment we are going through a period which is madly destructive of one of the finest forms of cinema. The 'spaghetti' has killed the Western!

10: L'Aîné des Ferchaux

It was in 1961, after Léon Morin, Prêtre *opened, that you signed the contract to film Simenon's* L'Aîné des Ferchaux.

Fernand Lumbroso, who owned the rights to the book, had signed a contract with Alain Delon. Delon had imposed the director of his choice, then he announced that he no longer wanted this man and Lumbroso began to look around for someone else. But when Delon sent him a registered letter reminding him that if no director was set for the film by a certain date the contract would be considered void, he cried off.

At this point Belmondo's agent, Blanche Montel, telephoned me to say that Belmondo had been offered *L'Aîné des Ferchaux* and wouldn't do it without me. An hour later, Lumbroso was asking to meet me, and when we got together he asked if I had read the Simenon novel. I said yes, but since he looked as though he really didn't believe me, I asked him whether he'd like me to describe the book or the film. Surprise followed disbelief, and eventually he said 'Describe the film.' So I described one of the possible adaptations of the book – one I did in fact write but didn't use. We signed the contract immediately.

Eventually I did an adaptation of *L'Aîné des Ferchaux* which was practically an original script: the Vanel character was no longer called Ferchaux, Belmondo wasn't Michel Maudet, and the title of the film was no longer *L'Aîné des Ferchaux*. But Fernand Lumbroso, who had paid sixteen million francs for the rights to the book and had already signed several contracts with distributors, begged me to go back to an intermediate stage. At that time I could still be swayed by such arguments.

In August 1962, immediately after shooting *Le Doulos*, I began *L'Aîné des Ferchaux*, editing and mixing the first film while shooting the second. I was working eighteen hours out of twenty-four. I was more dead than alive.

But you have always defended the principle of fidelity to literary sources.

I always insist on being faithful to the *spirit*. *L'Aîné des Ferchaux* is absolutely faithful to Simenon while deviating completely from the novel. I could almost say that the film is more Simenon than the book, though it's still a very Melvillian film. Where I deviated absolutely was in the relationship between Michel Maudet and Dieudonné Ferchaux, but this didn't stop critics from basing their reviews on my admirable fidelity to Simenon – which suggests that none of them had actually read the book. The thing I regret most is that I agreed not to change the names of the characters. Had I held out, the producer and distributor would have had to use my original title: *Un Jeune Homme Honorable*.

Why did you choose Charles Vanel to play Dieudonné Ferchaux?

To tell you the truth, I wanted Spencer Tracy, and in fact he had accepted, but the insurance companies wouldn't cover him because he was already very ill at the time. Charles Boyer was also very interested in the role, but he wasn't old enough, and anyway he was too good-looking for the part. So by default I came to Charles Vanel, because I thought he was a great actor.

Did you get on well with him?

Not terribly. We had a clash almost immediately. A silly clause in his contract made me furious and I ended up by being rude to him . . . which I regret, because I shouldn't have done it. Vanel's agent had put a paragraph into his contract which said something like, 'We hereby authorize you to ask for any changes you may think fit relating to your own role or those of the actors playing opposite you, either in dialogue or action scenes.' In other words, Vanel was in effect to be my supervisor. When I heard this, I got mad. 'If that's your contract,' I said to Vanel, crumpling it up, 'you can stuff it up your arse!' And I made him telephone his agent on the spot to remove the clause in question. And I refused to return to the set until the matter had been settled.

And how did you find Michèle Mercier for the part of Lou?

I'd seen her in several films and thought she was beautiful. You know that shot in *Tirez sur le Pianiste* where she is showing off her breasts? Truffaut shot it for me. She's great, that girl. She hasn't had the career she deserves.

Why did you introduce a boxing-match into the film?

In the first place because I'm very fond of boxing; it's a sport I practised when I was young. But also because I wanted to be the first director to use Belmondo in the role of a boxer.

Contrary to what people think, Belmondo didn't get his broken nose in the ring but in the army. What happened was that during his military service he broke his nose with a rifle in order to get his discharge. But it is true that Belmondo knows how to box. The referee for the fight in the film was his boxing instructor. His opponent, who was also his double, was a real boxer, Auzel, formerly a French champion. As a matter of fact, without meaning to he really did knock

Belmondo out: the second time you see him fall, it's for real.

That fight is also a *hommage* to Robert Wise's *The Set-Up* and to Herman Melville's *Moby Dick*, because I have Belmondo's voice off saying 'If we had won tonight . . .' and the first words of the commentary are 'Call me Michel Maudet . . .'[1]

In losing this fight, does Michel Maudet also lose his youth?

Absolutely. From that moment his whole life is in the balance. During his walk along the Boulevard Auteuil – which replaces Simenon's Paris to Caen train journey – he even finds the courage to throw away the red beret that he's clung to as a reminder of his past as a parachutist. He's a man of the Right, is Michel Maudet.

The first time we see Dieudonné Ferchaux he's in the boardroom at a directors' meeting. The scene suggests another Robert Wise film : Executive Suite.

Yes, of course. That scene – which I shot at the rue Jenner – enabled me to dispose of a large chunk of Simenon's novel which didn't interest me at all. When I have Dieudonné Ferchaux say, 'Let's forget the details,' that takes care of a good hundred pages of the book.

What exactly does Dieudonné Ferchaux represent in the film?

Do you really not know? Even if I remind you that I made the film in 1962? Don't you read the newspapers? Don't you remember an American personality who disappeared in 1961? Howard Hughes! In 1961, up to his ears in litigation with the State, Howard Hughes suddenly disappeared after hiring a secretary at the last minute. For five years no one – not even the FBI – could find out where he was. He reappeared only when he was no longer liable for the financial operations he

1. The French title of *The Set-Up* is *Nous Avons Gagné ce Soir* ('We won Tonight'). The opening sentence of *Moby Dick* is 'Call me Ishmael . . .'

had been conducting. So my Ferchaux is Howard Hughes.

Michel Maudet and Dieudonné Ferchaux often resemble each other . . .

Yes, and the resemblance is more than hinted at in the scene in the bank when they go to get the money. The way they walk is identical, and you'd think they were of the same stock. They are two of a kind.

Where did you shoot that scene in the bank?

In a bank.

Yes . . . but what I meant was, in France or in America?

In America. Why? You look as though you didn't believe me.

Not at all . . .

Well, you shouldn't. As a matter of fact I shot that scene at the Société Générale in the Boulevard Haussmann, because all banks look alike.
    I discovered one day that Monsieur Vanel wanted to take advantage of the film to spend his honeymoon in America. So I deprived Monsieur Vanel – and consequently Belmondo – of America. I was therefore obliged to shoot certain exteriors in France: the sequence with the hitch-hiker, the scene at the river, and so on. Not that this prevented the American Tourist Office of the United States Embassy from sending me a letter of thanks and congratulation for the way I had shown the Appalachians, and in particular the bridge over the river.

What is there of America in the film, then?

Only things that are typically American and where I didn't need Vanel or Belmondo in shot. Obviously I didn't film the streets of New York in the rue Jenner, but all the scenes on the highway were shot in France. If you look carefully, however, you will see that none of the cars are French, because I'd lined the Esterel autoroute with American cars.

Your film is a wonderful sort of love story between a disappointed old man and an ambitious young one.

Dieudonné Ferchaux is an old man who suddenly, faced with youth in the person of his companion, effects a transference. Michel Maudet is young, and the love he feels for him is pure narcissism. Being physically attracted by Maudet, Ferchaux begins to fall in love with him. The fact that he discovers for the first time at the age of seventy that he is capable of homosexuality drives him completely crazy, which is why he behaves like an old woman with his fits of despair and jealousy.

Rather than a meditation on old age, my film is first and foremost a meditation on solitude. Don't forget what Ferchaux says to Maudet in the cabin at New Orleans: 'Tonight, you served your apprenticeship in freedom, Michel . . . and I mine in solitude.'

It's in the fight with the two Americans that Ferchaux discovers youth in Maudet?

Precisely. It's because of the fight that Ferchaux looks at Maudet's hands in the next scene when he's driving the car. They please him. The hands in the shot are my own. While I was at the wheel, Decaë sat inside and also filmed the landscape as it went by. For the shots in which the two actors appeared, I used back projections, because as I said they didn't come to America.

You always explain your characters through their behaviour, which leaves a good deal of room for ambiguity.

Nothing is ever definitive about the way a man is or seems,

because he must change. He is constantly evolving. Of course, the good or the bad in his character will not disappear over the years, but the way he behaves must necessarily be modified by his life. At the age of fifty, a man will certainly not reason the way he did at twenty, thirty or forty.

I detest Manicheism. I don't believe that it corresponds to any reality today in 1970, at least where people who live in towns are concerned. I believe that there are, among the people who still live close to nature, some who are really good. But I don't believe that city-dwellers, people destroyed by the towns, are still capable of goodness.

Among the exteriors you shot in America there is a neon sign for the Holiday Inn motels which carries the legend 'Pray for Peace'.

We shot that scene at the beginning of November 1962, just when war almost broke out between America and Russia over Cuba. Through that sign I was able to convey the feeling in America at the time.

When Kennedy learned that there were Russian missiles in Cuba, he had to know before sending a message to Khrushchev whether the Russians would or would not back down if faced by the threat of war. So, at three o'clock in the morning, he summoned representatives of all the great computer firms to the White House; and after assembling all available information (data about genuine military resources, desire for peace, fear and so on), they fed it into their computers. Four hours later, all of them came up with the same answer: the Russians, faced by a threat to bomb Cuba, would withdraw their missiles. And the machines were right!

That was the night I filmed 'Pray for Peace', while telling Decaë, 'Tomorrow we may be plunged into the Apocalypse again.'

Why did you decide on the song Sinatra sings in Capra's A Hole in the Head *for the film?*

All Sinatra's songs don't belong to Sinatra. I wanted to use 'What Is This Thing Called Love?', but according to American union rules I would have had to pay for the entire orchestra. The same thing didn't apply to the song in the Capra film, because Sinatra was accompanied by an orchestra of non-union children.

How did you find the house where Sinatra was born?

With great difficulty. It took an enormous amount of research to find the record of his birth – which proves, incidentally, that he is older than you think – and that led us to his place of birth. The window you see in the film is the window of the room where he was born.

In Simenon's book, Maudet killed Ferchaux and sold his head to Suska, the Dutchman who shrank human heads to sell to tourists. Why did you abandon this grim ending?

Because I couldn't live for a year with a man capable of selling Dieudonné Ferchaux's head. It might be interesting to read, but it would have become intolerable on the screen.

Have you ever met Georges Simenon?

Oh, no! The moment I discovered that Simenon is one of those people who never see the films adapted from their books, the last thing I wanted was to meet him. I can be just as disdainful as he can. He doesn't interest me as a person. This said, however, some of Simenon's books have given me great pleasure.

In the film you never show the signs announcing the names of the towns you passed through with the camera.

No, I didn't want to show them. But I can tell you that when

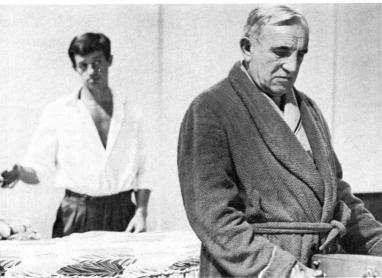

L'Aîné des Ferchaux: Malvina, Jean-Paul Belmondo, Andrex; and (*below*) Belmondo with Charles Vanel

you see Belmondo's back through the window of the cabin as he disappears into the forest (it's my assistant, Georges Pellegrin, doubling for Belmondo), this is at Melville, near Baton Rouge.

At one point, however, I do show a sign which bears the legend 'De Beauregard St. Stop!' This warning was intended for de Beauregard, to tell him he'd go bankrupt if he wasn't careful. But he didn't heed the warning . . . !

Near the end of the film, Maudet is preparing to abandon Ferchaux, taking the suitcase of money with him, when the old man says brokenly, 'Brutus killing Caesar. But you're no Brutus.' To which Maudet's cutting reply is, 'And you, you old carcass, do you think you're still Caesar . . . ?'

It's the final confrontation between the two men. There is nothing more to be said, and Maudet leaves, flinging a contemptuous 'Ciao! Adios!' at the old man after hissing 'Tragediante, commediante!'

But Maudet is more faithful than he thinks. When he returns with the suitcase, though, it is to stand helplessly by at the death of Ferchaux, who gives him the key to the vault at Caracas before he dies. Touched by this gesture, Maudet cannot conceal his emotion. The last line of the film seems to contradict this new feeling of his : 'To hell with you and your key . . .'

What I like about this scene is the tenderness which comes through it. The expression in Maudet's eyes belies the words he speaks. Don't forget that Maudet is a Melvillian hero.

11 : Le Deuxième Souffle

How did you first become interested in Le Deuxième Souffle?

The novel had been kicking around producers' offices in France ever since it was published in April 1958. Because it consisted of two stories which had no connection with one another, it was practically impossible to adapt and no one wanted to buy it. The author had been after me for years to turn his book into a film. I invariably replied that first of all I had to find the 'idea'. 'The idea? What idea?' he asked me once. 'The idea which will enable me to link up the two stories,' I explained.

And then one day I at last found the solution. I brought Orloff in at the beginning of the film (in the novel he made his first appearance on page 104), so as to dovetail the Marseilles story with the Paris story, one within the other.

You were originally going to make Le Deuxième Souffle *in 1964 with an entirely different cast, weren't you?*

I was going to make the film with Fernand Lumbroso, the producer of *L'Aîné des Ferchaux*. Serge Reggiani was to be Gu; Simone Signoret, Manouche; Lino Ventura, Blot; Roger Hanin, Jo Ricci; Georges Marchal, Orloff; Raymond Pellegrin, Paul Ricci. All the contracts were signed, but the whole thing collapsed. I even sued everybody . . . it's a very complicated story.

In the version Denys de La Patellière was then supposed to make, Jean Gabin was Gu, and Lino Ventura retained the role of Blot. La Patellière summoned the young actor I had engaged to play Antoine to offer him the same part, only to be told, 'No. I was supposed to act in Monsieur Melville's film and I don't want to be in yours.' I much appreciated this reply, which revealed the attitude of a man who knew his own mind. The speaker? Pierre Clémenti! I shall repay him one day . . .

Why didn't you use him in 1966?

Because he wasn't available. I replaced him with Denis Manuel – who is in fact very good in the film. You must remember that the decision to film *Le Deuxième Souffle* was taken in four days. I started shooting on 21 February 1966, and on 17 February nothing had been decided. This explains why I used Marcel Combes as lighting cameraman. He had telephoned me a few days previously, and as I had nobody to hand and all the cameramen I wanted weren't available, I engaged him.

But his camerawork does no disservice to the film . . . quite the reverse.

That's true, but I had to do everything myself, and I assure you that having to look after the photography as well as direct is rather exhausting. We continued working until 14 March in extremely difficult conditions and then had to stop for three months. When we started again on 7 June, it seemed like a miracle.

1964 to 1966 were years in the wilderness for me.

What are the basic differences between Bob le Flambeur *and* Le Deuxième Souffle *in your opinion?*

There is absolutely no connection between the two films. *Bob*, for me, is not a thriller but a comedy of manners. In it I take no account of the war or the Gestapo, and the *milieu pourri* exists only in Bob's words. *Le Deuxième Souffle* is a *film noir*.

The differences between the book and the film are enormous.

If you attempt to catalogue the differences you'll have enough material to fill your entire book. Had I filmed the novel, I would have ended up with *Un Nommé La Rocca*.[1] There are a lot of things in it which are just padding. The author has not created a work of imagination: he has simply written down stories told him in jail by his fellow prisoners. It's a total recall of everything he learned in prison; the dossier on one of those legendary heroes, the Charrières-Papillons, whose exemplary lives are turned into stories. On this level *Le Deuxième Souffle* is a very interesting book; an absolutely authentic document on the Marseillais *milieu* which gave birth to the rue Villejust Gestapo. But this is not my province as a film-maker: as you know, I never deal in realism. So I retained what was Melvillian from the book, and threw everything else out. If a good director were to remake *Le Deuxième Souffle* tomorrow, forgetting my film and sticking to the novel, he would end up with a typical French film. Remember, for instance, that we first meet Orloff in the brothel run by Yvette; that Venture (Paul in the film) Ricci has a completely dim wife called Alice; that Poupon, Blot's assistant, spends his time running after girls; and so on, and so on. The book ends, with Gu only just dead, with Orloff and Manouche kissing each other. Can't you just see the kind of film it would make? So I pride myself on having made a completely original work.

What were the differences between the Gestapos of the rue Lauriston and the rue Villejust?

The seven Paris Gestapos were all formed in the same way.

1. Another novel by José Giovanni, filmed by Jean Becker in 1961 with Belmondo and Pierre Vaneck.

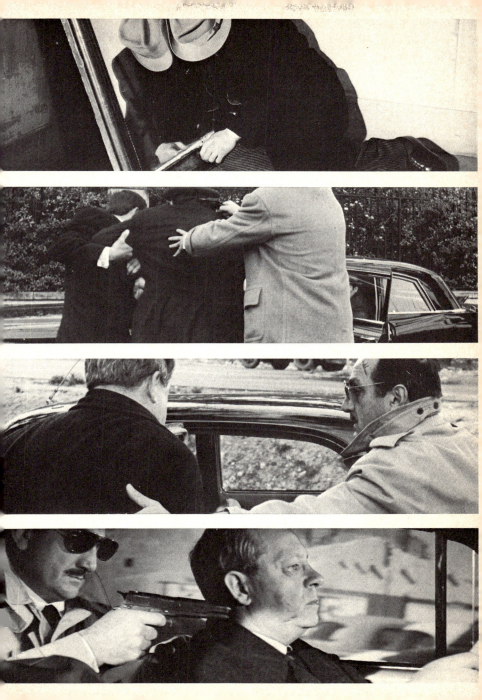

We've already mentioned the most famous one, the rue Lauriston, which included Abel Danos, who is the Abel Davos of *Classe Tous Risques*.[1]

The rue Villejust Gestapo was the Parisian section of the Corsica/Marseilles Gestapo, and gave rise to a famous joke during the war. There is a knock at the door. The frightened occupants ask 'Who's there?' And from behind the door, a voice replies in a thick Corsican accent, 'German Police.'

In your films policiers people spend their time 'doubling' each other, while the hero reacts like a jackal or a wounded tiger. Why?

Because if there are two of you, one betrays. Why do you think I have chosen solitude? (*Laughter.*) Commerce with men is a dangerous business. The only way I have found to avoid being betrayed is to live alone. Do you know two men who have lived and worked together as good friends and who are still on amiable speaking terms a few years later? I don't. Friendship is a sacred thing, like the existence of God for those who believe in it. As soon as you realize things 'aren't going too well', it opens the way to all kinds of betrayal. I believe that betrayal is one of the basic motivations behind men's actions – much more than love. Love is what makes one live, they say in *Carmen*. It isn't true. It's betrayal.

Do you think friendship is an illusion you lose as you grow older?

Yes, but I'm a tremendous believer in friendship . . . in my films! When you are young, you think that men are interesting animals. I have no illusions any more. What is friendship? It's telephoning a friend at night to say, 'Be a pal, get your gun and come on over quickly' – and hearing the reply, 'O.K., be right there.' Who does that? For whom?

Until he is thirty-three, a man is convinced he'll always be twenty years old. Then one day he looks at himself in the mirror and sees that the years have gone by . . . The realization

1. Also adapted from a novel by Giovanni: directed by Claude Sautet in 1960, with Lino Ventura and Belmondo.

that one is growing old is tragic. It means understanding suddenly that one is alone. Old age is the consummation of solitude.

Your characters are much more 'regular guys' than their real-life counterparts, aren't they?

Certainly. The real inhabitants of the *milieu* don't interest me. In actual fact the *milieu* is as rotten as the bourgeoisie. Why should it be better?

Is deceit a form of intelligence – or a means of self-defence – that you particularly admire?

In my films or in my life? In the cinema, any means of capturing the audience's interest is valid. I approve of deceit in so far as it's a device for making images or situations interesting. In real life, on the other hand, I don't like it at all. I'm not saying that I systematically condemn man's baser instincts, because I am a man like the rest, no better and no worse. I accept this human condition with all that it implies: I imagine, therefore, that I have been deceitful on occasion, though I couldn't tell you when. But I'd like to quote you something that was said to me a year ago by Pierre Braunberger, a man who knows the film world backwards: 'Basically,' he said, 'you are the only case I know of success through intransigence. You have always said "No!", you have never cheated. You have behaved like a brute, and you've still succeeded . . !' So presumably I'm not deceitful, because an old pro like Braunberger would have noticed. My mentality is more that of a bulldozer: I think the shortest distance between two points is a straight line.

In this underworld you bring so marvellously to life, one must kill or be killed. Is this the way you see the world today?

Oh, no, you're on the wrong track again. You mustn't try to interweave what I do in my films with what I am in life. You know very well who I am in life: a man living in a solitude for five – my wife and three cats – who has made it an absolute rule not to associate with his contemporaries. I have a friend like Jan de Hartog, whom I think of as a brother but whom I never see: there he is on his island in Florida, and here I am at Tilly. There is no question of having to kill or avoid being killed all the time. No one wants to kill me, and I don't want to kill anyone. I ask only one thing in life: to be left in peace. I spend my time leaving other people in peace. Don't ever think, even if I sometimes feel strongly about the things I tell you, that there is any connection between me and my characters. I tell stories that interest me, or which, transposed, recall a period of my life. But they are never personal stories. Never! Never! Never! It is true that there is a scene in *L'Armée des Ombres* which relates to my private life; but it's the only one and it only lasts two minutes.

There is always a marked mutual sympathy between your crooks and your policemen.

It really exists, that mutual sympathy. On the radio once, when I pressed him, Commissaire Letallanter of the crime squad admitted it: 'With an intelligent crook who has made a confession, who speaks frankly and stops playing about, you often find a sort of fraternization between him and the police officer . . .'

After the shooting in the restaurant which causes the death of Jacques-le-Notaire, you have Blot's curious speech, done in a single shot. How did you film this scene?

I sent Paul Meurisse back to his dressing-room because he was very worried at the thought of doing a scene like that in a single shot, and then went on the set to rehearse in his place. I acted out the whole of this sequence which marks the first appearance of Blot, at the same time pointing out each camera position to my operator, Jean Charvein, while my chief grip traced out the camera's exact path on the floor. It was only after planning every last detail of the scene that I brought in the cameraman to arrange his lighting. Then, when everything was ready, I sent for Paul Meurisse and told him just to do anything he liked. 'What? Anything I like?' He was absolutely amazed, because he knew how difficult the scene was. 'Yes, do anything that seems logical to you.' And I swear he did exactly what I had done . . . He had to, because I had anticipated every move, and I also knew my actor.

You manage to obtain from your actors not only a very spare acting style but a particular kind of diction and intonation.

This is because I write my own dialogue, and the lines are conceived to be spoken at the speed with which I speak. So my actors mustn't have a quicker or slower delivery than mine.

I'm a great believer in the direction of actors. There is no doubt that it is directing in two stages – which is very hypocritical – that enables me to get the right delivery and performance from each actor. The first time, I shoot with direct sound recording. Then I take each actor separately and make him dub himself in an auditorium watching a loop of film which confronts him endlessly with his own image until he feels a sort of nausea. It's difficult to make an actor dislike himself, but when he sees himself making the same face ten, fifteen or twenty times over, his defences are weakened and I can take him in hand. It's at this point that I can get him to say his lines as I want.

In the book Gu and Manouche make love, but their relationship in the film is rather ambivalent. Manouche is even referred to as Gu's sister . . . although 'sister' means 'mistress' in the milieu, doesn't it?

'Sœur' and 'Frangine' ['sister' and 'little sister'] are both used by crooks to refer to their women. If I've let it be understood that Manouche is Gu's sister, it's because of the *Enfants Terribles* part of me – or rather, because of the great homonym's *Pierre or the Ambiguities*.

Is Blot in love with Manouche?

Not in love, but it is possible that there has been something between them. That is why I made them use the familiar 'tu' when they are alone in the office. As soon as Godefroy (Jean-Claude Bercq) comes in they restore the proprieties and use 'vous'.

The preparation and execution of the hold-up are brilliant.

In the book the hold-up was introduced in a few sentences, but for me this is the crucial part. In the pre-hold-up, unfortunately, there is a reel-change over some very important frames relating to the pursuit of the van by the Mercedes, which no one ever sees because projectionists are so afraid of missing the change-over that they always swallow some images. Basically, though, it's my fault because it was a bad cut. I made the same mistake as John Ford in the scene in *The Long Voyage Home* where Thomas Mitchell looks at Ward Bond's body as it disappears. There are some effects which die at reel-ends.

The scenes with the motor-cyclists who are killed were very difficult to shoot because at the last minute I didn't get the stuntmen I was expecting. I had two good motor-cyclists but they weren't stuntmen. I could hardly kill them, so I had to cheat the scene. The results are very good, even so. The scene with the van going over the cliff I shot with four cameras because there was no question of doing it a second time. Two cameras were up on the plateau on a little rocky promontory – in the hope that the van would turn back on itself, which it did – and another in a boat out at sea.

Le Deuxième Souffle: The hold-up

After the hold-up, Antoine's admiration for Gu knows no bounds . . .

After seeing Gu at work, Antoine is completely under his spell and would be ready to follow him anywhere. This scene is the celebration of a masterpiece executed by two old-world craftsmen. They have done what they had to do. But Antoine, a professional killer, is not intelligent; and when he is told that Gu has double-crossed them, he believes it. Antoine is the beat generation; a slightly Nouvelle Vague crook, perhaps, but his kind have always been around. I also gave him a touch of individuality by having him say he is a gipsy and cross himself before killing the motor-cyclist.

But although Gu and Antoine are real professionals, they take unnecessary risks . . .

Antoine does it through pride: to prove his skill, he removes the telescopic sight from his rifle. With Gu, it's an act of defiance: he uses the same revolver with which he has killed before. Gu, of course, knew that he was already finished. But his gesture needlessly sacrifices Paul, Antoine and Pascal.

Gu betrays the names of his associates under the impression that he's talking to another gang. When he realizes he has been tricked by the police, he knows it's all over; from that moment he knows that only death can redeem him.

At the beginning of the film, when Manouche learns of Gu's escape, she says, 'Ten years ago I wanted to help him; I was even afraid he might kill himself.' So Gu is already finished when the film begins. He's had a ten-year reprieve, you might say.

In the book it's Blot who disguises himself as a crook to make Gu talk. I used the cop played by Négroni because he looks a little like the George Raft-style Italian gangster. I had him powdered and made up like the Neapolitans so that he'd look like an old-time gangster – because before the war some crooks used make-up, though it had nothing to do with homosexuality.

When Négroni asks Lino Ventura for the names of his accomplices, I wanted the latter's reply to come in two stages: first he would shake his head, and then he would say 'No!' I thought the gesture followed by this one simple word would strengthen the scene. Ventura didn't agree (he felt it wasn't how he would do it in real life) and was determined to underline the 'No' by shaking his head. I forced him to do it my way, telling him that in my films people don't behave as they do in real life. Ventura was so angry that if you watch the scene carefully, you can see his carotid artery pulsing as the zoom brings his face into close-up. But that same evening he telephoned to say I was right . . . he must have been rehearsing the scene in front of his mirror before calling me.

You had problems with censorship over some of the torture scenes?

When I showed the film in the complete version, people couldn't look at the screen. The scene where a cop sticks a funnel into Paul Ricci's mouth and pours water into it from a can really was unbearable. Even though the cut doesn't damage the film too much – as it stands the scene gives free rein to the spectator's imagination – I still think it's a pity it *was* cut. But I must make it clear that I was not under orders from the censors. The President of the Commission simply advised me not to retain this scene because it might cause me some bother.

When Gu shaves off his moustache, and when Blot drops the notebook with Fardiano's confession, both of them are committing suicide . . .

Absolutely. They stop trying to fight it. Gu stops hiding. Blot

123

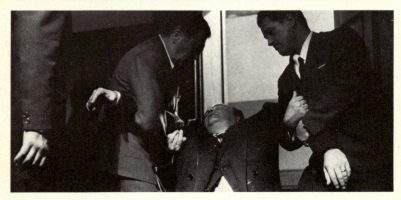

Le Deuxième Souffle: Raymond Pellegrin in the torture sequence

resigns from the police – through respect for Gu, perhaps. As a matter of fact they often use the same gestures.

Putting a cigarette between their lips without lighting it, for instance . . .

It's the same cigarette, in effect.

Why did you have engravings of Napoleon in Paul Ricci's office?

Because Raymond Pellegrin, who plays Paul Ricci, had appeared as Napoleon in Sacha Guitry's film. I once did a whole series of photographs of Pellegrin dressed as Napoleon because I was planning to film *La Mort du Duc d'Enghien* with him as Napoleon. But then Sacha came along . . . Pellegrin got the part because of my photographs.

12 : Le Samourai

What was your starting-point for the script of Le Samourai?

An idea for an alibi. A man commits a crime in the presence of eye-witnesses, yet remains unperturbed. Now, the only alibi you can really count on in life is one backed up by the woman who loves you . . . she would rather be killed than give you away.

I liked the idea of beginning my story with a sort of meticulous, almost clinical, description of the behaviour of a hired killer, who is by definition a schizophrenic. Before writing my script, I read up everything I could about schizophrenia – the solitude, the silences, the introversion. Do you remember Lacenaire? Delon in *Le Samourai* is a little like Marcel Herrand in *Les Enfants du Paradis*, except that the latter kills in his own interests.

For a schizophrenic, theft is an indispensable complement to murder. Jeff Costello steals the car so that his act will be more complete. In a crime effected in two stages, there is always a sort of plateau of reflection between the first and the second. Jeff Costello is neither a crook nor a gangster. He is an 'innocent' in the sense that a schizophrenic doesn't know he's criminal, although he *is* criminal in his logic and his way of thinking.

I was careful not to make him a parachutist washed up after

Le Samourai: Alain Delon as Jeff Costello, 'by definition a schizophrenic'

127

the war in Indo-China or Algeria who had been taught to kill for his country! Jean Cau liked *Le Samourai* a lot. Although he didn't know me at all he was so convinced that I had drawn a self-portrait that he began to psychoanalyse me even as he was telling me he knew nothing about analysis. He explained all my unconscious intentions, and I must say he managed to build an absolutely hallucinating portrait of me.

Le Samourai is the analysis of a schizophrenic by a paranoiac, because all creators are paranoiac.

Years ago I read a very fine novel by Graham Greene, *This Gun for Hire*, which was filmed by Frank Tuttle with Alan Ladd, but there were great gaps in the portrait of the schizophrenic. In the same way *Pickpocket*, which is a film I love, doesn't quite come off. Is it perhaps the dialogue that's wrong? I'm inclined to think so, because it doesn't ring true.

But with Bresson this element of falseness in the dialogue is deliberate.

Yes I know, and that's where I'm not Bressonian – sorry, a Bressonite. Bresson's characters never express themselves in a manner I can accept. On the other hand I always love their gestures and the motivation behind their actions. *Pickpocket* is a marvellous failure.

Why did you risk such a new departure as Le Samourai *after the success of* Le Deuxième Souffle?

When I contacted Delon to offer him Lesou's *Main Pleine* – this was before Deville filmed it – he sent me a completely idiotic letter typed on an IBM President in which he said he couldn't consider my proposal because he had a series of much more important projects for the immediate future in America.

So when in his turn he contacted me after the success of *Le Deuxième Souffle* to say he would be happy to make a film with me, I sent him the Lesou book without telling him it had now been filmed under the title of *Lucky Jo*, and said 'We're going to do the film you turned down three years ago.' After reading the book, he agreed. But it was impossible to get the rights again, so I offered Delon the role of Gerbier in *L'Armée des Ombres*. He refused, but asked if I hadn't another script I wanted to do. In 1963, before he told me he was bucking for an international career, I had written an original script for him. I told him this and he immediately insisted that I read it to him.

The reading took place at his apartment. With his elbows on his knees and his face buried in his hands, Alain listened without moving until suddenly, looking up to glance at his watch, he stopped me: 'You've been reading the script for seven and a half minutes now and there hasn't been a word of dialogue. That's good enough for me. I'll do the film. What's the title?' '*Le Samourai*,' I told him. Without a word he signed to me to follow him. He led me to his bedroom: all it contained was a leather couch and a samurai's lance, sword and dagger.

The line from the Book of Bushido *with which you open the film – 'There is no greater solitude than that of the Samurai, unless perhaps it be that of the tiger in the jungle' – might apply equally well to your situation as an independent film-maker outside the industry . . .*

Absolutely! Do you know that the film was shown in Japan complete with that opening title which I attribute to the *Book of Bushido*? What they don't know is that I wrote the 'quotation'.

The treatment of colour in Le Samourai *is very different from* L'Aîné des Ferchaux.

Whereas the colours in *L'Aîné des Ferchaux* are very warm, I wanted very cold colours for *Le Samourai*. With this in mind I carried out a series of conclusive experiments, which I carried even further in *L'Armée des Ombres*, and further still in *Le Cercle Rouge*. My dream is to make a colour film in black and white, in which there is only one tiny detail to remind us that we really are watching a film in colour. I think we took a small step forward in a form of expression – cinema in colour – which has become dangerous. You can hardly work in black and white any more. No producer would risk three or four hundred thousand dollars when television is only interested in colour films.

Even during the credit sequence, the first shot of Delon stretched out on his bed conveys the impression of the solitude of the 'samurai'.

My intention was to show the mental disorder of a man who unmistakably had a tendency to schizophrenia. Instead of simply resorting to the now almost classical technique of a track back compensated by a zoom forward, I used the same movement but with stops. By stopping the track but continuing the zoom, then starting the track again, and so on, I created an elastic rather than classical sense of dilation – so as to express this feeling of disorder more precisely. Everything moves, but at the same time everything stays where it is.

When Delon gets up from the bed, do you feel we are seeing death set in motion?

Yes, of course, because man carries his own death within him. But Death is personified in the film by Cathy Rosier . . . with whom Delon falls in love.

To get into Jeff's room and place the microphone there, the police use exactly the same method he uses to steal the car : a bunch of keys on a wire ring.

Le Samourai: Jeff as 'the wounded wolf': Jeff with the 'Death personified' he falls in love with (Cathy Rosier); and the final scene in which the Inspector (François Périer) shows her that Jeff's gun was unloaded

That's because I wanted to use in a dramatic film the Chaplin principle of showing the same thing three times in order to get a reaction from the audience. When they see this key-ring for the third time – as Jeff steals his second car behind the Châtelet, in other words – the audience reacts.

The first time Delon steals the car, though, one is moved. Seeing his lost expression through the rain-streaked windscreen, you are on his side at once.

I think we are with him before then . . . from the moment he strokes the birdcage with the bundle of banknotes. But with the shot you mention, we move inside the character.

When Jeff catches the eye of the girl in the car alongside, why doesn't he acknowledge her smile?

This contact illuminates the fact that Jeff is a schizophrenic. A normal man would have followed the girl, or at least smiled at her. But Jeff remains impassive because nothing can deflect him from his mission. The ritual theft of the car is the first act in his crime.

Why 'ritual' theft?

Because with schizophrenics every act is a rite. As a matter of fact, ritual itself is schizophrenic – make no mistake about that. I start from the principle that all animals are mad. Look at my three cats: there is always a ritual to their movements and actions. Since humans are animals, why shouldn't they be mad too? Ritual is an animal habit and therefore a human one, particularly in connection with religion. Like faith, it is part of the madness of man.

When he goes to get the number-plates changed on his stolen car, Jeff Costello drives full speed down that little back street and turns straight into the very narrow doorway of the garage. How did you shoot these scenes?

Because both the street and the door of the garage were so narrow, I told Delon just to pretend to drive the car in and I would cheat the scene later. A moment or two later, Delon drove the first car up at top speed, turned, and shot it in. With the second car he repeated the operation just as casually (the clearance was a centimetre, no more, between the car and the doorway). This is the superman side of every star. Top professionals don't need to be told how to hold a glass or smoke a cigarette: they have a sure, unshakeable instinct for the right gesture.

A star – I love that American definition – is an ordinary person with something else extra. That 'something else extra' is indefinable: it shows in the direct, dynamic impact of a star on the public. The craft of acting can't be taught: either you're gifted or you're not. Lino Ventura, for example, has never been taught how to say lines, but he does it better than anybody.

The part of the garage mechanic is played by André Garret, who worked with you once before as Roger, the safe-cracker in Bob le Flambeur.

Yes, he was an old friend. Although he was very ill, he agreed to do this small part in *Le Samourai* to please me. After the shooting was finished, he just had time to dub himself before going into hospital to die. When he says, 'I warn you, Jeff, it's the last time,' he knew he was dying. Delon learned of his death the day he came to record his reply to this line, and his 'All right' is spoken like a farewell.

As with Gu and Manouche, the relationship between Jeff Costello and Jeanne Lagrange is rather obscure. Why exactly did you cast Nathalie Delon – who was then Delon's wife – as Jeanne?

Nathalie and Alain look like brother and sister: *Pierre or the Ambiguities*. It was a sort of instinct that made me give the part to Nathalie, because originally I wanted her to play the pianist. With her temperament I felt she must be a woman on whom a man could depend; that if ever she had to give evidence on Alain's behalf she would acquit herself splendidly. Events have proved that I was right. I'm very fond of Nathalie: she's a marvellous girl, completely open and with great character. She's unimpeachable. A rock. Water can batter away but it has no effect.

When they meet for the last time in Le Samourai *and Delon kisses her hair, he closes his eyes. Did you tell him to play the scene like that?*

Yes. And every time I look at that scene now, I get the impression that they're saying goodbye for real . . . in fact it was that same evening that they finally separated.

At one point Jeff says, 'I never lose, not really.'

These words reveal his lucid grasp of his own destiny. He knows that as long as he lives he will win. Only death can make him a loser – as it inevitably must, and Jeff falls in love with his death. Cathy Rosier, a black Death in white, holds the charm that fascinates, captivates . . .

Jeff meets her for the first time while carrying out his first contract, the assassination of Martey. Their eyes meet, but she is unafraid . . .

At that moment Jeff has the hypnotic power of the serpent which just stares at its prey until it can no longer move. Sure of his power, he prevents her from crying out just by looking at her. He dominates Death because he is not yet subject to her.

Unlike Gu, who uses the same gun twice, Jeff throws his revolver into the Seine after killing Martey.

Careful! Gu isn't a professional. Given the circumstances in which he finds himself he has to kill, but he isn't a killer. He's a gangster who knows he's reached the end of the line. Jeff is a pro, as they say in America.

During the police raid on the room where they're all playing cards, you can hear somebody saying, 'I'm a war pensioner – 100 per cent disability.'

I had the line spoken by a foreigner, a man with a very strong accent . . . it's something I dredged up out of my memory. It's quite common to hear things like that said by guys playing cards in the hotels around Barbès when the police make a raid; and they're always said by the Marcantonis – people with fantastic service records. I knew a Gestapo killer who wore the insignia of the Médaille du Combattant in his buttonhole.

Monsieur Wiener, the character played by Michel Boisrond, says he has no sense of observation; yet he gives a perfect description of Jeff . . .

Wiener is the 'gentleman friend' who pays the rent. He has known for a long time that the girl he's keeping has a lover, he knows his name and what he looks like. In spite of their rivalry, there is always a *modus vivendi* between the gentleman friend and the fancy man. Jeff, understanding the psychology of men like Wiener, arranges his alibi in two parts, counting on the spirit of revenge. So Wiener, intending to incriminate him, exonerates him.

In Le Deuxième Souffle, *Blot says to Jo Ricci, 'I think all the time; that's what I'm paid for.' But the police inspector in* Le Samourai *says to his assistant, 'I never think.'*

The Périer character is much more crafty and intelligent than the one played by Meurisse. Périer is a police chief with a big D. He is Destiny. Beneath his average-Frenchman exterior, the Périer character has a Cartesian mind, and he also has great intuition. He refuses to accept Jeff's watertight alibi: he lets him go but he has him followed. My point is that the policeman who says 'I never think' is the one who thinks the most. A policeman is a man, and therefore a liar.

When the police go to see Jeanne Lagrange and ring her bell, she calls 'Is that you, Jeff?' The voice that answers 'Yes' sounds astonishingly like Jeff's.

Of course, because I used Delon's voice for the purpose. This is one of those small dishonesties essential to every creator. Creative art is based on lies – which can only be exploited properly, in my opinion, if one is not a liar in real life.

So you agree with Jean-Marie Straub when he says that no one can be considered a master of the cinematographic art unless his life and morals are beyond reproach?

Absolutely. Artistic creation, especially in the cinema, demands an exemplary life to compensate for the craziness and disorder it entails. I am not a saint, nor am I particularly virtuous, but I believe that undue disorder in one's daily life excludes all possibility of creativity. I could cite specific examples to support this theory.

There is evidently a sort of understanding between Jeff and his pet bird.

Jeff and the bird love each other. They are on the same wavelength. I wanted the opening shots to be predominantly grey, so I used a female bullfinch because it is just black and white, without the male's orange breast. She burned along with my studio.

When Olivier Rey and his men are discussing Jeff, one of them says, 'He's a lone wolf,' but someone else says 'No, a wounded wolf.'

A lone wolf is the animal most likely to defend itself against the dangers . . . of the Great White North, let's say, like in Jack London. When a lone wolf is wounded, he becomes more dangerous but is considered to be finished. See Dix Hanley in *The Asphalt Jungle.*

Why does Jeff, who is very level-headed, nevertheless return to the scene of the crime?

He knows he's not running any risks – which is why he also throws the packet of blood-stained dressings away in the street. He simply wants to show the pianist – through his serpent's eye – that he wants to meet her. When the crooked barman says to him, 'If you were the man the police are looking for, one could say that the murderer always returns to the scene of the crime,' Jeff doesn't like the remark and goes to wait for the pianist outside.

You make the barman say exactly what the audience is thinking when it sees Jeff going into the bar again.

That was intentional. One should always undermine that sort of effect. I'll give you an example. One evening my wife and I went to see an excellent play by Anouilh, *La Grotte.* A couple of minutes after the play began I turned to Florence and said, 'Pirandello!' Just at that moment, an actor on stage said, 'I have just heard someone in the audience say "Pirandello".'

The policemen who go to hide the microphone in Jeff's room behave exactly like crooks.

They are the minions of the illegal house-search. No police

force will ever admit to having special duty squads for this kind of work. I present these men as petty officials doing their 'duty' with the assurance which comes from having the law behind you. Apart from this assurance, only one tiny detail reveals that these men belong to the police: when they leave in their car, I have them set off the wrong way down a one-way street. No one ever notices the traffic sign, however, because the scene isn't brightly enough lit.

We never learn exactly who Olivier Rey is.

Originally he was the head of the French Secret Service. Then, because of various spy films, I changed the script and Olivier Rey became something or other in an anonymous organization. Actually, I don't know who Olivier Rey is, I don't want to know, and I don't want anybody else to know . . . He is the MacGuffin Hitchcock talks to Truffaut about.

The tailing sequence in the Métro, controlled by those police communication devices, is a veritable manhunt.

Commissaire Letallanter of the Paris crime squad – in other words the man who does Périer's job in real life – said to me when he saw the film, 'That's a great idea of yours . . . If we were given the resources to set up tailing jobs like that, our task would be a lot easier . . .'
    As the action proceeds, the tailing becomes more and more difficult. The rhythm is set by the montage. Montage is the heartbeat of a film.

This poem of yours dedicated to the land of Mizoguchi closes with Jeff Costello's death, one of the great hara-kiris *of the cinema. Jeff is completely expressionless when he dies, but I have seen some production stills where he has a smile on his lips.*

Actually, I shot the scene with and without the smile. I used

Le Samourai: The alternative version of Jeff's death

the second version, although the first was the one in the script.

Why does Jeff put on white gloves before executing a contract?

White gloves are a tradition with me: all my killers wear them. They are editor's gloves.

In the last shot of the film, everyone leaves the nightclub and the lights go out. Is this to say 'The show is over'?

Yes. That's why I had the drummer tap 'pim, pam, pom'. When a session ends the drummer always takes his sticks and taps on the side drum (pim), the 'Charleston' (pam) and the cymbal (pom).

13 : L'Armée des Ombres

When did you first read Kessel's book?

I discovered *L'Armée des Ombres* in London in 1943 and have wanted to film it ever since. When I told Kessel in 1968 that my old dream was going to come true at last, he didn't believe anyone could pursue an idea so tenaciously for twenty-five years.

Although you have been very faithful to the spirit of the book, you have again made a very personal film.

For the first time in this film I show things I have known and experienced. Nevertheless my truth, of course, is subjective and has nothing to do with actual truth. With the passing of time we are inclined to recall what suits us rather than what actually happened. The book written by Kessel in the heat of the moment in 1943 is necessarily very different from the film shot cold by me in 1969. There are many things in the book – wonderful things – which it is impossible to film now. Out of a sublime documentary about the Resistance, I have created a retrospective reverie; a nostalgic pilgrimage back to a period which profoundly marked my generation.
  On 20 October 1942, I was twenty-five years old. I had been in the army since the end of October 1937 . . . behind me were

three years of military life (one of them during the war) and two in the Resistance. That leaves its mark, believe me. The war period was awful, horrible and . . . marvellous!

So the quotation from Georges Courteline with which L'Armée des Ombres *opens is a reflection of your own feelings – 'Unhappy memories! Yet be welcome, for you are my distant youth.'*

Precisely. I love that phrase and I think it's extraordinarily true. I suffered a lot during the first months of my military service, and I thought it hardly possible that a man as witty, intelligent and sensitive as Courteline could have written *Les Gaîtés de l'Escadron*, whereas of course he too had been very unhappy during his service. Then one day, thinking over my past, I suddenly understood the charm that 'unhappy memories' can have. As I grow older, I look back with nostalgia on the years from 1940 to 1944, because they are part of my youth.

I believe that L'Armée des Ombres *is considered a very important book by members of the Resistance.*

L'Armée des Ombres is *the* book about the Resistance: the greatest and the most comprehensive of all the documents about this tragic period in the history of humanity. Nevertheless, I had no intention of making a film about the Resistance. So with one exception – the German occupation – I excluded all realism. Whenever I saw a German I always used to think, 'Whatever happened to all those Teutonic Aryan gods?' They weren't the blond, blue-eyed giants of the myth; they looked very much like Frenchmen. In my film I ignored the legend.

Did you have a technical adviser for the German uniforms?

I saw to everything myself with the assistance of my costume-designer, Madame Colette Baudot, who was very well documented on the subject. One day while we were filming the shooting-range sequence, the French army captain who was responsible for the technical side of it told me that there was something wrong with the SS uniforms. So I summoned my costume-designer and the captain said to her, 'I am from Alsace, Madame, and during the war I was forcibly enrolled in the SS. So I can assure you that a member of the SS always wore an arm-band on his left arm with the name of the division he belonged to . . .' 'No, Sir,' Madame Baudot replied, 'you must certainly have belonged to an operational division, whereas the SS in the film are from a depot division.' And the captain was obliged to admit that she was right.

Some critics in France accused you of presenting the Resistance workers as characters from a gangster film.

It's absolutely idiotic. I was even accused of having made a Gaullist film! It's absurd how people always try to reduce to its lowest common denominator a film which wasn't intended to be abstract, but happened to turn out that way. Well, hell! I wanted to make the film for twenty-five years and I have every reason to be satisfied with the result.

The Resistance people themselves liked the film very much, didn't they?

Yes, I have had wonderful letters, and when I arranged a private screening for twenty-two of the great men of the Resistance, I could see how moved they were. They were all Gerbiers, Jardies, Félixes . . .

'As leader of the *Combat* movement,' Henri Frenay told me, 'I was obliged to return to Paris in December 1941 although I had no wish to see the city under occupation. I got out of the Métro at the Etoile station, and as I was walking towards the exit I could hear the sound of footsteps overhead . . . it was a curious feeling keeping in step with them. When I came out on the Champs-Elysées I saw the German army filing past in silence, then suddenly the band struck up . . . and you reconstructed the scene for me in the first shot of your film!'

For that scene, you know, I used the sound of real Germans marching. It's inimitable. It was a crazy idea to want to shoot this German parade on the Champs-Elysées. Even today I can't quite believe I did it. No one managed it before me, not even Vincente Minnelli for *The Four Horsemen of the Apocalypse*, because actors in German uniform had traditionally been banned from the Champs-Elysées since the First World War. One German was anxious to buy the footage from me at any price, because all they have in Germany is a black and white version of the parade.

To do this shot, which may well be the most expensive in the history of French cinema – it cost twenty-five million Old Francs – I was first of all given the Avenue d'Iéna for rehearsals. At three o'clock in the morning, with all traffic stopped and the Avenue lit exclusively by gas-lamps, men in uniform began to march past. It was a fantastic sight. Wagnerian. Unfilmable. I swear to you that I was overwhelmed. Then I was afraid . . . I began to wonder how it would go at six in the morning when I was shooting on the Champs-Elysées.

You know, of all the shots I have done in my life, there are only two I'm really proud of: this one, and the nine-minute thirty-eight-second shot in *Le Doulos*.

Where did you shoot the opening concentration-camp scenes?

In a former concentration-camp which was completely in ruins and which I partially reconstructed for the film. Alongside this old camp there was another, brand new, clean . . . waiting. It had been built two years previously. All over the world there are camps like this one. It's fantastic. Terrifying.

Physically speaking, the Commandant of the camp is very different from the one Kessel describes in his book.

Yes, mainly because I didn't want him to be unsympathetic. I made him a rather dry character, wearing the Pétain insignia – La Francisque – which distinguished the legion of French volunteers for the national revolution. The emblem of the Fascist Party, in other words.

Why in the film, unlike the book, are Luc Jardie and his brother Jean-François each unaware of the other's clandestine activities?

I wanted to avoid melodrama. You don't see it? You may be right, perhaps. But go and see *L'Armée des Ombres* in a local cinema. At the moment when the big boss comes down the ladder into the submarine and they realize that he is Jean-François's brother, the audience can't help going 'Aaaahhh!' The two brothers' failure to meet is made all the more remarkable by the fact that Fate is shuffling the cards for all time: shot under a false name by the Gestapo, Jean-François will die without ever knowing that Saint-Luc is the head of the Resistance, and Saint-Luc will never discover what happened to his brother. The circumstances make the disappearance of Jean-François all the more tragic.

Why, in the film, does Jean-François send the Gestapo the anonymous letter denouncing himself?

This is one of those things I never explain, or don't explain enough. When Félix meets Jean-François in Marseilles, he says, 'Well, still enjoying "baraka"?' When a man has 'baraka' – a divine grace bringing good fortune, according to the Arabs – he feels secure against adversity. Jean-François is not afraid to send the letter which will mean his arrest because he feels secretly convinced that he has enough 'baraka' to save Félix and get away himself. But he has only one cyanide pill . . . the one he gives to Félix.

L'Armée des Ombres: Images of the Resistance (Jean-Pierre Cassel, *above and centre*; *below*, Simone Signoret)

There was no coal left during the war, and fuel oil wasn't used for heating in Paris. So apartments were freezing cold, especially in old houses with huge rooms; and people built these little wooden living-spaces to go inside rooms, where they could eat or read and be more or less sheltered. You can't imagine what life in France was like at that time. People often slept fully dressed, shoes and socks included, because there was nothing one could do about the cold.

Things weren't much better where food was concerned. Hunger became an obsession. You thought of nothing else. I can still remember the indescribable joy I experienced one day when I managed to make a sort of sandwich with lard and garlic. In the mornings, to get the circulation going, we would drink a kind of old sock juice made out of roasted peas. Because I didn't want to make a picturesque film about war, I didn't go into any of these details.

As the story proceeds, my personal recollections are mingled with Kessel's, because we lived the same war. In the film, as in the book, Gerbier represents seven or eight different people. The Gerbier of the concentration camp is my friend Pierre-Bloch, General de Gaulle's former Minister. The Gerbier who escapes from the Gestapo Headquarters at the Hôtel Majestic in Paris is Rivière, the Gaullist Deputy. As a matter of fact it was Rivière himself who described this escape to me in London. And when Gerbier and Jardie are crossing Leicester Square with the Ritz Cinema behind them advertising *Gone With the Wind*, I was thinking of what Pierre Brossolette said to me in the same circumstances: 'The day the French can see that film and read the *Canard Enchaîné* again, the war will be over.'

Why did you remove all the details explaining why the young man, Dounat, becomes a traitor?

To explain them would have been to detract from the idea of what a betrayal means. Dounat was too weak, too fragile . . . he reminds me a little of the young liaison officer – he was fifteen years old – we had at Castres for the *Combat* movement. One day I had been warned by Fontaine, the Political Commissioner for Vichy, that the Gestapo were preparing a raid, and I sent him to warn the Resistance group at Castres. Although he assured me he was carrying no compromising papers, a sort of instinct made me search him and I found a notebook full of addresses. A few moments later he got himself arrested by the Germans.

Despite his position, Commissaire Fontaine was a genuine Resistant. Later, he too was arrested. He was deported and never came back.

What did you do during the war before you went to London?

I was a sub-agent of BCRA and also a militant with *Combat* and *Libération*. Then I went to London. Later, on 11 March 1944, at five o'clock in the morning to be precise, I crossed the Garigliano below Cassino. With the first wave. At San Apollinare we were filmed by a cameraman from the U.S. Army Cinematograph Service. I even remember acting up when I realized we were being filmed. There were still Germans at one end of the village, and Naples radio was playing Harry James's *Trumpet Rhapsody*.

I was also among the first Frenchmen to enter Lyon in uniform. Do you remember the spot where the scene between Gerbier and Mathilde takes place, beside the pigeon-house? It was there, on that little Fourvière promontory belonging to the bishopric, that I arrived in a jeep with Lieutenant Gérard Faul. Lyon lay at our feet still full of Germans. We left that same evening after installing an observatory on Fourvière's little Eiffel Tower . . . When I think of everything that happened in those days, I'm amazed that the French don't make more films about the period.

Do you know when I saw Faul again? One Sunday morning in February 1969: the day I had the German army marching through the Arc de Triomphe. When the scene was in the can I went to the Drugstore des Champs-Elysées with Hans Borgoff, who had been Bandmaster of the 'Gross Paris' during the four years of the Occupation, and whom I had brought from Germany to come and help me shoot this scene. While I was breakfasting with the man who used to march every day at the head of the German troops, I recognized an old young man sitting near by as Lieutenant Faul, the man under whose orders I had fought the whole campaign in Italy and in France. Twenty-five years later the wheel had come full circle.

Why did you interpolate the scene where Luc Jardie is decorated in London by General de Gaulle?

Because in Colonel Passy's memoirs there is a chapter about the award of the insignia of Compagnon de la Libération to Jean Moulin, and Luc Jardie is based, among others, on Jean Moulin. Also I thought it would be interesting to show how de Gaulle decorated members of the Resistance in his private apartments in London so as not to jeopardize their return to France.

Does the hotel room in London mean something particular to you?

It's an exact reconstruction of the hotel room given to every Frenchman who came to London on business concerning the Resistance. Which means that every time I meet a member of the Resistance, he asks how I knew what *his* room was like.

You end the film with an announcement of the deaths of the four leading characters. Is this what actually happened?

Of course. Like Luc Jardie, Jean Moulin died under torture after betraying one name: his own. Since he was no longer able to speak, one of the Gestapo chiefs, Klaus Barbie, handed him a piece of paper on which he had written 'Are you Jean Moulins?' Jean Moulin's only reply was to take the pencil from Colonel Barbie and cross out the 's'.

A lot of people would have to be dead before one could make a true film about the Resistance and about Jean Moulin. Don't forget that there are more people who didn't work for the Resistance than people who did. Do you know how many Resistants there were in France at the end of 1940? Six hundred. It was only in February or March 1943 that the situation changed, because the first Maquis date from April 1943. And it was the proclamation by Sauckel (the man in charge of foreign labour and who introduced forced labour) about sending young people to Germany that made a lot of people prefer to go underground. It was not a matter of patriotism.

How did Kessel react to your film?

Kessel's emotion after the screening of *L'Armée des Ombres* is one of my most treasured memories. When he read the words announcing the deaths of the four characters, he couldn't prevent himself from sobbing. He wasn't expecting those four lines which he hadn't written and which I hadn't put into the script.

Do you think the film was well received in official circles?

I don't know. I was at a screening at the Ministry of Information before an audience which included everybody who was anybody in the Parisian smart set. Among the two hundred people present there was only one Resistant, and he was the only one to remain transfixed in his seat after the screening. It was Friedman, the man who, one night in April 1944, killed Philippe Henriot at the Ministry of Information.

Do you remember the moment in *Le Deuxième Souffle* when

'Today you are Gerbier!': Lino Ventura and the railway lines of *Le Deuxième Souffle* (*left*) and *L'Armée des Ombres* (*right*)

Lino Ventura crosses the railway line after the hold-up? When we shot that scene, Lino said to me, 'I've got it, Melville. Today I am Gu!' 'No,' I told him, 'today you are Gerbier!' It took me nine years to persuade him to accept the role. When we shot the scene in *L'Armée des Ombres* where he crosses the railway line in the early morning, we hadn't been on speaking terms for some time, but I am sure that at that moment he was thinking of what happened at Cassis railway station while we were filming *Le Deuxième Souffle*.

14: Le Cercle Rouge

How do you feel about your twelfth film, Le Cercle Rouge?

Since there is no knowing there will be a thirteenth, I must try to talk about *Le Cercle Rouge* as though it were not only my latest film but my last. Which in turn obliges me to speak about my film-making career as a whole as well as my career as a spectator. Maybe I won't want to make any more films. That could happen, supposing fate decreed that I wasn't to be allowed to rebuild my studios here, and I decided to go to live in America, to give up film-making and devote myself to writing. All that could happen, so I really am obliged at this juncture to take stock of twenty-five years of professional activity and some forty-five years activity as a spectator. I shall begin by being hard on myself before moving on to other people. Afterwards I'll talk about the film, but I'm also going to talk about what it's like working on a film surrounded by people who haven't at all the same reasons for being involved in it, for living it, while it's being made.

All right, then. If I look at myself very objectively, I recognize that I have become *impossible*. Not egocentric (I am not in the least egocentric), but – if I may be allowed to coin a word – opocentric ('opo', from *opus*). As I grow older, in other words, nothing matters except my profession and therefore my work, by which I mean the work on hand, which

I think about day and night and which takes precedence over everything, repeat *everything*, else in my thoughts . . . I am not talking about my affections, of course. So, I begin thinking about the film I'm working on as soon as I wake up in the morning – and I'm always working on one, even if I'm not actually shooting – and only when I go to sleep at night do I stop thinking about it. That's pretty extreme, and I was made aware of it last night. I was having dinner with Léo Fortel, and at the next table were two girls and two young men, who were later joined by a third. One of the two men was obviously a French Indo-Chinese . . . and opposite him was a ravishing girl, I think she must have been a half-caste, with extraordinary hair – probably a wig, pitch-black, worn Jeanne d'Arc style but longer – and the most fantastic face. I was staring at her throughout the meal, but when Léo asked me if I wanted him to find out her name and address, I said no. 'All right,' he said, 'but why not?' 'Well,' I said, 'I've no film in mind for her.' And I realized that beautiful women interest me only in so far as I think I can use them in a film. You see how far it's gone?

Well, I said just now that in growing older I had become very difficult, in both senses of the word: I am difficult to please because I am very exacting, and I am difficult with people because they find it hard to tolerate me as I am: my disposition, my defects, and this disease of perfectionism which attacks a conscientious film-maker as he grows older. I have become a perfectionist while the people I work with have, over the last twenty-five years, gradually become less so. Out of this twenty-five years experience, in other words, comes a positive impression that twenty-five years ago there were great people in the French crews; and that these people have become considerably less great. I say 'these people' because of course there are younger men now whom I don't know; and I'm talking about sound technicians as much as lighting cameramen or operators.

All this was even more evident on *Le Cercle Rouge*. This

film is by far the toughest job I have tackled, because I didn't do myself any favours in writing my scenes. I said to myself, 'This is going to be difficult to shoot, but I don't care, I want to do it.' And I did manage to film what I had written. But instead of completing it in forty-five to fifty days, which would have been normal, it took me sixty-six days, and this was because the men working with me . . . the men and the woman on set with me . . . just weren't up to it. It's all the more painful for me to have to say this – knowing that it is going to be set down in a book and become a sort of definitive statement – in that with me on the film was a man I loved very much, and still do love, who was my first collaborator. First not only in the chronological sense, but first in quality, in closeness, in complicity about ideas, technique and experimentation. Just now I said I had succeeded in shooting what I had written. Yes, but at what a price! What a price, I mean, in terms of fatigue, of driving the crew, of constantly struggling to avoid being worn down or crushed by this mass rather like a jelly-fish on a beach which moves only when someone moves it. I was able to move it only at the cost of absolutely superhuman efforts which I have never had to make before on any of my films – and they have by no means always been easy.

A few words about the problems I have nowadays in animating a French crew – keeping it alive, one might almost say – and I'll end my recriminations. I never used to have to make this effort a few years ago; even *L'Armée des Ombres*, which was also a very difficult film to shoot, didn't cost me half the worry and exhaustion that this one did. And this loss of professionalism, this lack of conscience, was evident in almost every department. One exception was the set decorator: he's the guy whose job it is to find all the props and furnishings, and his selections were always first rate . . . I don't think I had to turn down one important item – a few minor things, maybe, but nothing of consequence. His name, and I can't repeat it often enough, is Pierre Charron. He's the best set decorator in the French cinema, and believe me that counts in a film.

The second man who gave me full satisfaction – I'm sorry if I seem to be distributing prizes now – was Albouze, the props man. This was the first time I had worked with him and I had never met him before, but he's a great props man, the best I've ever had. (Charron I had worked with before on *Le Doulos*, and I'd tried to get him again on various other films but he was never free.) They were both perfect, and now I can pay tribute to both of them. It's marvellous to be able to say of someone that you have nothing to reproach him with, and with those two I can say it. But they're the only ones. As for the rest . . . From now on, I think that the people I can work with will be those who put their work before their private lives.

What is *Le Cercle Rouge*? *Le Cercle Rouge*, to my mind, is first and foremost the story of a robbery. It's about two professional crooks, played by Delon and Gian Maria Volonté, and another man, played by Montand, who comes to their assistance as a sort of accidental auxiliary.

As I've told you, I wanted to write a robbery script long before I saw *The Asphalt Jungle*, before I'd even heard of it, and well before things like *Du Rififi chez les Hommes*. I think I also told you that I was supposed to make *Rififi*? No? Well, I was the person who got the producer to buy the rights, he announced that I was to direct the film, and then I didn't see him again for six months. Finally the film was made by Dassin, who had the extreme courtesy to say that he would do it only if I wrote to tell him that I was happy about the arrangement. Which I did.

So I have wanted to 'do a robbery' since about 1950, around the time I finished *Les Enfants Terribles*. I'd like it to be masterly, of course, but I don't know yet if it will be; I think the elements are sufficiently interesting to make a good sequence, and time will tell if I have placed the robbery in the right context or not. It's also a sort of digest of all the thriller-type films I have made previously, and I haven't made things easy for myself in any way. For instance, there are no women in the film; and it certainly isn't taking the easy way out to make a thriller with five leading characters, none of them a woman.

A few years ago I tried to list all possible variations on my favourite cops-and-robbers situation, and I came up with nineteen. Not twenty, but exactly nineteen. Now, I have used all nineteen situations in my five thrillers – *Bob le Flambeur*, *Le Doulos*, *Le Deuxième Souffle*, *Le Samourai* and *Le Cercle Rouge* – but I have never used all of them in one film. However, there is a film, *The Asphalt Jungle*, which did use them all, and this was the film which enabled me to do my research into these nineteen possible situations. I'm telling you this because yesterday and the day before I saw a new Huston film called *The Kremlin Letter*, and it's a masterpiece. As we left the cinema, I said one word to my wife: 'Masterly!' Masterly, the work of a master, a teacher, and *The Kremlin Letter* could serve as a lesson in cinema. I'm delighted to see a man like John Huston, who already has so many great films behind him, returning to the front rank.

Is Le Cercle Rouge *one of the twenty-two scripts which disappeared when your studio burned down?*

No. Actually, with my memory, I could have selected one of those scripts and rewritten it down to the last comma. But if I had I would have done it differently. I don't like to repeat myself. I shall never film those burned scripts, because I wouldn't want to do them now even if I still had them in my drawer – which doesn't mean that I won't often use ideas from those scripts, as I in fact did for the relationship between the Inspecteur Général des Services and Commissaire Mattéi in *Le Cercle Rouge*.

The *Cercle Rouge* script is an original in the sense that it was written by me and by me alone, but it won't take you long to realize it's a transposed Western, with the action taking place in Paris instead of the West, in our own time rather than after the Civil War, and with cars replacing the horse. So I start off with the traditional – almost obligatory – conventional situation: the man just out of jail. And this man is near enough the exact equivalent of the cowboy riding behind the titles who pushes open the saloon doors as soon as the credits are over.

Originally you planned a different cast for the film, didn't you?

Yes. Commissaire Matteï, who is played by André Bourvil – and played beautifully – was a part originally intended for Lino Ventura. The ex-cop Jansen, turned crook and sodden with drink, was to have been played by Paul Meurisse, and not Yves Montand. And I had thought of offering Belmondo the role of Vogel, now played by Gian Maria Volonté. I think that if Delon hadn't wanted to do *Borsalino* with Belmondo, I would have got them both together in *Le Cercle Rouge*. I regret that it didn't happen. But every film is what it is, and it stands or falls by its own merits. It's a moment out of one's life, a film. In my case at least, you must remember, it represents fourteen months of uninterrupted work crammed into twelve – 1968 was a completely wasted year for me, because I had signed a contract with the Hakim Brothers to make *La Chienne* and they managed not to honour it. They made me lose a whole year immediately following the fire at my studios, which was a terrible blow in a lot of ways; because losing the studios and all they represented in terms of money and opportunities was bad enough, but then to be reduced to twelve months of unemployment by a contract retaining exclusive rights over your services and preventing you from doing anything else whatsoever – that *is* a terrible blow. Hence the fourteen months of work crammed into twelve, because in 1966 I made *Le Deuxième Souffle* (begun on 7 February), in 1967 I made *Le Samourai*, in 1968 I did nothing, in 1969 I did *L'Armée des Ombres*, and in 1970, *Le Cercle Rouge*. Well, when you reach my age, you are entitled to think that a film is

156

an important thing in your life, because it represents at least a year's work and then dogs you for another year: you remain the man of last year's film, or of your last film to be shown. So in fact a film may be said to take up two years of your life. A film is what it is, whether it stands or falls, and I am quite sincere when I say that I have no regrets – quite the contrary – about not being able to get the actors I originally wanted for three of the leading parts in this one.

In the shooting script for Le Cercle Rouge, *when Commissaire Matteï is trying to recapture Vogel after his escape, you have him say: 'He isn't Claude Tenne. I couldn't ask the Home Secretary to block every road in France.' Who is this Claude Tenne you refer to?*

Claude Tenne was a member of the OAS, and during the Algerian crisis he was tried and sent to jail for his activities against the Government. He managed to escape from the Ile de Ré where he had been imprisoned by folding himself into four and hiding inside a military canteen, a sort of big iron trunk, though not so very big actually – I have no idea how he did it. And at the time all the roads in France were blocked.

At another point in the script, you describe Jansen as follows: 'Jansen, stretched out on his bed, fully dressed, filthy, unshaven, with a three-day beard. Like Faulkner in one of his alcoholic bouts.'

Yes, I imagine Faulkner or Hemingway as being like that in their bouts of alcoholism. As a matter of fact I believe there are many eyewitness accounts of how Faulkner sometimes used to stay shut up in his room with his bottles for a week with orders that he wasn't to be disturbed.

But Jansen's hallucinations – rats and spiders crawling slowly towards him – are the sort of nightmares Edgar Allan Poe might have dreamed up?

157

Well, of course. You know that Poe and Melville have a great deal in common . . . But now I'm getting mixed up, forgetting when I say Melville that it's not me but the great . . .

You admire Herman Melville enormously, yet he never accepted the idea that one must grow old and die. You, on the other hand, seem to face the prospect with great serenity.

You surprise me: I'm not so sure that Melville was afraid of growing old and dying. Are you certain that this is historically true? I can't see that it's particularly evident in his work. Is it because a century has passed since then, and that now we accept these things more readily? I think growing old is a marvellous, exciting thing; the only trouble is that it suddenly stops being like that, and once it has become something terrible you haven't so very long to prepare for the coming of death. In this context you ought to read the admirable interview with François Mauriac in *L'Express* this week (9 May 1970). I think Melville and I have a great deal in common, which is probably why I have been under his spell ever since my adolescence, although nowadays I also feel myself drawing very close to Jack London.

Who was a man of the Left . . .

Unlike the person you take me to be? In the first place, I'm not so sure he was Left wing. I think he was a man of the Right with Socialist ideas – something far more common than you'd think. My reason for thinking so is that when he talks about the Indians, for instance, he does so in exactly the same way as he talks about dogs or wolves; and when he talks about the Indians as a race apart, I think you can take it that there is a little bit of racialism in him in spite of everything; and racialism, as we all know – or at least as everyone tries to have us know – belongs to the Right, like all unhealthy attitudes. But Jack London was a man of genius. Do you really think it's possible for a man of genius not to be full of perpetual, permanent contradictions?

Are you a man of the Right?

Well, it amuses me to say so, because everyone else claims to be Left wing, and that irritates me. I hate following the crowd, and in any case to say that one is wholly Right or Left wing is ridiculous . . . I don't think it's possible. Philosophically speaking, my position in life is extremely anarchistic: I am an extreme individualist, and to tell you the truth I don't wish to be either Right or Left. But I certainly live as a man of the Right. I'm a Right wing anarchist – though I suppose that's a barbarism and that no such thing really exists. Let's say that I'm an anarcho-feudalist. Anyhow, although I may be Right wing some of the time, I can't be all of the time, because I am very well aware that it isn't the Right which is going to do anything about the misery of those members of the human race who are cold, hungry, suffering, enslaved or oppressed. So conscience stirs strongly enough within me to know that even if I oppose the Left – or those who call themselves the Left – I can't really be Right wing, basically and deep down. It isn't possible. I think if I was fundamentally Right wing, I couldn't make the films I do make. It was, of course, Soviet Russia that dispelled any illusion I had about the Left being synonymous with virtue. Thirty years ago my political ideal, it goes without saying, was Socialism. I was a Communist then as a matter of fact. Then suddenly, on 23 August 1939, Communism began to frighten me. I realized that the war which was to break out on 3 September 1939 . . . perhaps I should tell you that on 3 September 1939 I felt like committing suicide because I realized that this war was one which was going to blow everything sky-high, and that it was the will of a Communist that had started it. It was Stalin, on 23 August 1939, who declared that war was going to break out . . . the day he agreed with Germany to parcel out Poland. And that day my Communism – my Socialism – suffered a severe blow. Then I began to think that the Siberian labour camps – whose existence was known before the war, though we didn't yet know about the extermination camps – formed part of Lenin's Socialist principles. So I changed. But I still say, as I suggested just now while talking about Jack London, that it is wrong to criticize people for being weathercocks and changing direction. It is life, and not your own will, that changes you, turns you into a completely different person.

Furthermore, I'm wary of any political credo, and I have no religious beliefs whatsoever. So what I have left is morality and . . . conscience. The first and only article in my personal code is very simple: 'Do nothing to injure your neighbour.' I really do try not to bother anybody by the way I live. And I really do believe I've succeeded.

'My freedom ends where my neighbour's begins . . .?'

Well, no, I don't entirely agree . . . because my liberty subsumes the liberty of my neighbour, and I respect it absolutely. I would do nothing to harm him, but as a last resort I might arrange to have no neighbour. Which, as you will have noticed, I have done both in this house where we are now and in my country home. I bother nobody, and in bothering nobody I have also arranged things so that nobody can bother me.

What are your future projects?

The film I want to make is the film I'll want to make as I'm making it. I'm no longer at the stage where I can say I want to do a particular film: that's a young film-maker's game, I think, and I'm no longer a young film-maker. For me, the cinema is a sacred thing, and it's the ceremony, the service celebrated during the shooting, that governs everything else – although, as you know, I rate the conception, scripting and editing more highly than the actual shooting. But there is no doubt that the shooting is the altar, and everything else is the vestry, because it's at the moment of shooting that a quasi-religious ceremony is celebrated between the director and the star which is in a sense rather like a marriage. Though it often happens that my stars and I aren't on very good terms during shooting, the sacrament of our relationship still persists, because one can marry and hate and still retain the complicity of mutual understanding.

I have made two films with Alain Delon, and it's marvellous because we have an extraordinary complicity during shooting. This is offset – since everything must be offset by something or other – by the extraordinary complexity of his character. But at the same time you could say that these moments of complicity and communion are enriched by the fact that his life is so complicated, that he is subject to fits of depression, and that he isn't always completely at your disposition – or at least he wasn't for *Le Cercle Rouge* because the old scandal was still dragging on, because he was the producer on *Borsalino*, and because he was having personal problems with Belmondo, who didn't collaborate very actively on publicizing the film. Actually, it's rather amusing to see how Alain can be a star behaving like a star, and at the same time behave like a producer because he has produced a film.

You have drawn up a sort of critical balance-sheet for your technicians; would you care to do the same for your cast?

All right. I have already told you about my excellent relationship with Delon during shooting and the extraordinary personal complicity which enables us to work in a very special way. This is the first time I have worked with Yves Montand, who is a very fine actor, but his music-hall background gives him a training very different from any Delon may have had. Delon is enormously gifted and doesn't need as much preparation as Montand, who is a perfectionist like me. Montand is the sort of actor who arrives on set in the morning with the

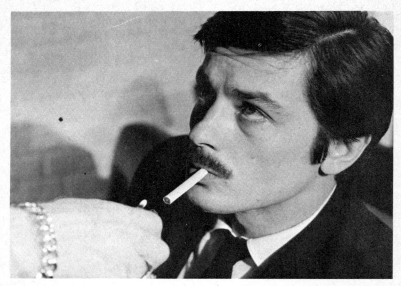

Le Cercle Rouge: 'A sort of digest of all the thriller-type films . . .'

whole thing in his head. Everything went off beautifully with him too – he's enormously willing and dedicated. If you want proof, consider what he's just been doing in *L'Aveu*. This man, known to the whole world as a Communist, has had the courage to accept the role in *L'Aveu* of a character who accuses the Communist régime of having committed inconceivable crimes; and I do mean inconceivable, because it was easy enough to attribute every sort of vice to the Nazis or the Fascist régime in general, but less easy for the pre-war Left to imagine that similar crimes could be acceptable to a Socialist régime. Anyhow, it was marvellous working with Montand, and I hope to make many more films with him. In the first place because he's a man of about my age – he's three years my junior, actually – so he's easier for me to use as a vehicle than a much younger actor. Alain and Jean-Paul, let's say, are vehicle-characters for me because they are thirty-five years old, and if I give Delon a moustache, that's it, he's a man, not just a nice young man, but a man. Handsome, maybe, but it doesn't matter because it no longer gets in the way. Anyway, to my mind, Montand is also handsome.

André Bourvil is an excellent actor, one of the best in France, but he probably isn't *a priori* a Melvillian actor. I think he gives a very interesting performance in my film, and I'm all the more convinced of this after going through the whole film again on the cutting-table: there are moments where André Bourvil is absolutely staggering. In his case I'm very happy about the casting change, because Bourvil brings an element of humanity to the part which I hadn't expected and Lino Ventura certainly wouldn't have had. Lino Ventura would have been 'Le Commissaire', and there would have been no surprises; whereas with André Bourvil – thanks to André Bourvil – there are quite a few[1].

As to François Périer, everyone knows he's one of the great French actors and there's really nothing more to be said. I remember the evening I met you outside a cinema where they were playing *Le Samourai*, and we both exclaimed together,

1. André Bourvil died in 1970 after this interview took place.   163

'Périer is fantastic!' This film can only add to his reputation. The astonishing thing, though – and it's one of the distressing aspects of this business – is that at this moment François Périer isn't rated as a star and he should be. This upsets me, just as it upsets me that Richard Boone isn't a star. But in this area it's still the distributor who lays down the law and not the film-maker. If you want to make films which are . . . I won't say ambitious, but serious and costing a fair amount of money . . . it isn't easy to use people who aren't stars in your leading roles. Distributors won't take the risk. They always say, 'No, no, think of the billing, use names, etc.' I think it's a pity you can't even think of making an expensive film, costing say a billion Old Francs, with unknowns. I could set up a film tomorrow with unknowns if it cost three hundred million, but not a billion. They will pay out three hundred million on my name because they know more or less what sort of product they'll get from me, but they won't give me more. The billion for *Le Cercle Rouge* was possible because I had Delon, Bourvil and Montand, and because there was a sizeable Italian co-production interest since I was using an Italian actor, Gian Maria Volonté – totally unknown in France, I might add – whom I'd had in mind to play Vogel after seeing him in Carlo Lizzani's *Banditi a Milano*.

But, if you want me to talk about Gian Maria Volonté, that's a very different story. Because Gian Maria Volonté is an instinctive actor, and he may well be a great stage actor in Italy, he may even be a great Shakespearean actor, but for me he was absolutely impossible in that on a French set, in a film such as I was making, he never at any moment made me feel I was dealing with a professional. He didn't know how to place himself for the lighting – he didn't understand that an inch to the left or to the right wasn't at all the same thing. 'Look at Delon, look at Montand,' I used to tell him, 'see how they position themselves perfectly for the lights, etc. etc.' I also think the fact that he is very involved in politics (he's a Leftist, as he never tires of telling you) did nothing to bring us together. He was very proud of having gone to sit-in at the Odéon during the 'glorious' days of May–June 1968; personally, I did not go to sit-in at the Odéon. It seems, too, that whenever he had a week-end free he flew to Italy to spend it there in what I would call a sort of super-nationalist spirit. I once said to him, 'It's no use dreaming of becoming an international star so long as you continue to pride yourself on being Italian – which is of no consequence, any more than being French is.' But for him everything Italian was marvellous and wonderful, and everything French was ridiculous. I remember one day we were setting up a back-projection scene and he was smiling to himself. I asked him why, and he said, 'Because . . . you've seen *Banditi a Milano*? There are no back projections in *Banditi a Milano*. Everything was shot direct from a car.' 'Really?' I said, 'And did you have night scenes like this? You were inside a car filming the action going on outside *at night*?' 'Well, no,' he said, and it seemed to sink in that we weren't using back projections just to amuse him. He's a strange character. Very wearying. I promise you I won't be making any more films with Gian Maria Volonté.

Can you draw any conclusions from these twelve films you have made since 1947?

In these twenty-three years, since I don't want to take things I did before into consideration – or let's say these twenty-five years, because after all it was in 1945 that I founded my production company: I was demobilized in October 1945, and formed the company on 5 November 1945 – in these twenty-five years of professionalism I have done many things. First, in 1947, I got the idea of building my own studios, which I did. At one point I was the only film-maker in the world to have his own studios. This period lasted from 1949, when I made *Les Enfants Terribles*, till 1967, or eighteen years in all, with a short break when I gave the studios up for a time before being able to rebuild them as I wanted. Then in June 1967, they

165

burned down. Nothing much remains, but I am rebuilding them, even though I haven't yet been granted permission to do so by the authorities in Paris. So parallel to the films I have made . . . well, in an article I received yesterday, there is a sentence that reads, '. . . the novel *Le Silence de la Mer*, which was adapted for the screen by the father of the new French cinema, Jean-Pierre Melville.' This was published in the Algerian newspaper *El Moudjahid*, and was written by the literary critic Ahmazid Deboukalfa. I don't know this man except by name, but I'm delighted to know that someone outside France remembers from time to time that 'it was Melville, after all, who turned everything upside-down in 1947.'

Then in 1957 I built a projection theatre on the rue Washington, and cutting-rooms as well, but since hiring out screening-time and cutting-rooms isn't my business, I sold my interest. However, I have always felt the need for some parallel creative activity, in building and materials, because cinema isn't created with ideas alone. There's the whole mechanical side of it, and of course projection. For instance, during the three years my studios were hired out to Pathé-Marconi, I couldn't stand not having my own projection theatre, so I built one which I rented out to other people but could use myself in the evenings to run through any films I wanted to see. This sort of thing will always happen with me. At the moment I'm in the process of ruining myself to create a projection theatre here in the rue Jenner which is going to be marvellous because if, for instance, Monsieur Cocteau of Fox were to lend me a print of *The Kremlin Letter* tomorrow morning, what a joy it would be to screen it here during the morning and then return it to the Balzac Cinema at 1.30 p.m. in time for the first show. Suddenly absolute bliss opens up: seeing films here in the best possible conditions, comfortably seated with no one in front of you, no one coming in or going out, no usherettes to bother you with their chattering.

I don't know what will be left of me fifty years from now. I suspect that all films will have aged terribly and that the cinema probably won't even exist any more. I estimate the final disappearance of cinemas as taking place around the year 2020, so in fifty years time there will be nothing but television. Well, I shall be happy if I have one line devoted to me in the 'Great Universal Encyclopaedia of the Cinema', and I think that's the sort of ambition every film-maker must have. This is a business in which you have to be . . . not *arriviste*, certainly not that, nor yet ambitious, which I'm not . . . but you have to have ambition in what you do, which isn't at all the same thing. I'm not ambitious, I don't want to *be* something; I have always been what I am, I haven't *become* anything; but I have always had, and I shall always try to retain, this feeling that ambition in one's work is an absolutely healthy, justifiable thing. You can't make films just for the sake of making films. If fate wills that I should make more films, I shall try to remain faithful to this ideal of being ambitious when I start a film; not being ambitious between films, but being ambitious when I start work, telling myself, 'This must give pleasure.' That's my ambition you see, to fill cinemas; and what I like about Costa-Gavras is that he has the same healthy ambition when he sets up and films *L'Aveu. Z* was a little different, more of a thriller, whereas *L'Aveu* doesn't make any concessions to anybody, and perfectly defines the sort of thing I'm talking about.

I take my hat off to him, it's a marvellous ambition. I'm sure John Huston had this same pure ambition when he set up *The Kremlin Letter*. And Huston is a good name to end with.

Filmography

Jean-Pierre Melville.

Born Paris, 20 October 1917
Educated at the Lycées Condorcet, Michelet, Charlemagne, Paris.

Features

Le Silence de la Mer (1947)

Production Company	O.G.C.
Producer	Jean-Pierre Melville
Production Manager	Marcel Cartier
Director	Jean-Pierre Melville
Assistant Director	Jacques Guymont
Script	Jean-Pierre Melville. Based on the novel by Vercors [Jean Bruller]
Director of Photography	Henri Decaë
Editors	Jean-Pierre Melville, Henri Decaë
Music	Edgar Bischoff
Musical Director	Paul Bonneau

Howard Vernon (*Werner von Ebrennac*), Nicole Stéphane (*The Niece*), Jean-Marie Robain (*The Uncle*), Ami Aroe (*Werner's Fiancée*), Denis Sadier (*SS Officer*), Heim, Fromm, Rudelle, Vernier and Max Hermann (*German Officers*), Georges Patrix, Henri Cavalier, Dietrich Kandler.

Filmed on location in and near Paris, and at Vercors' home, August 1947–December 1947 (twenty-seven days shooting in all). First shown privately, 11 November 1948; first shown in Paris, 22 April 1949 (previously at a *soirée de gala* organized by the Comité d'Action de la Résistance, 20 January 1949).
Running time: 86 min.

Les Enfants Terribles (1949)

Production Company	O.G.C.
Producer	Jean-Pierre Melville
Production Managers	Jean-Pierre Melville, Jacques Bralay
Director	Jean-Pierre Melville
Assistant Directors	Claude Pinoteau, Jacques Guymont, Michel Drach, Serge Bourguignon
Script	Jean-Pierre Melville, Jean Cocteau. Based on the novel by Jean Cocteau

Dialogue	Jean Cocteau
Selection and editing of narrative passages	Jean-Pierre Melville
Director of Photography	Henri Decaë
Camera Operator	Jean Thibaudier
Editor	Monique Bonnot
Art Director	Jean-Pierre Melville; sets constructed by Emile Mathys
Music	Bach's Arrangement in A Minor for four pianos of Vivaldi's Concerto in B Minor for four violins, Opus 3; and Vivaldi's Concerto Grosso in A Minor
Musical Director	Paul Bonneau
Sound	Jacques Gallois, Jacques Carrère

Nicole Stéphane (*Elizabeth*), Edouard Dhermitte (*Paul*), Jacques Bernard (*Gérard*), Renée Cosima (*Dargélos/Agathe*), Adeline Aucoc (*Mariette*), Maurice Revel (*The Doctor*), Roger Gaillard (*Gérard's Uncle*), Mel Martin (*Michael*), Jean-Marie Robain (*School Bursar*), Emile Mathys (*Vice-Principal*), Annabel Buffet (*The Mannequin*), Maria Cyliakus (*The Mother*), Rachel Devirys, Hélène Rémy, and the voice of Jean Cocteau.

Filmed on location in Paris, Montmorency and Ermenonville, at the Théâtre Pigalle and at the Studios Jenner, November 1949–January 1950. First shown in Paris, 29 March 1950 (previously at Nice, 22 March 1950). Running time: 107 min.

Quand Tu Liras Cette Lettre (1953)

Production Company	Jad Films/S.G.C. (Paris)/Titanus (Rome)
Producer	Louis Dubois
Production Manager	Paul Temps
Director	Jean-Pierre Melville
Assistant Directors	Pierre Blondy, Yannick Andrei
Script	Jacques Deval
Director of Photography	Henri Alekan
Camera Operator	Henri Tiquet
Editor	Marinette Cadix
Art Directors	Robert Gys, Raymond Gabutti, Daniel Guéret
Music	Bernard Peiffer
Guitar Solo	Sacha Distel
Sound	Julien Coutellier, Jacques Carrère

Juliette Gréco (*Thérèse*), Philippe Lemaire (*Max*), Daniel Cauchy (*Biquet*), Irène Galter (*Denise*), Yvonne Sanson (*Irène*), Jacques Deval (*The Judge*), Jean-Marie Robain (*The Notary*), Suzanne Hédouin (*Manageress of the buffet*), Robert Dalban (*The Barman*), Hélène Dana (*The Naked Girl*), Fernand Sardou (*Garage mechanic*), Philippe Richard (*The Butcher*), Léon Larive (*Clerk of the Court*), Marcel Delaître (*The Grandfather*), Jane Morlet (*The Grandmother*), Suzy Willy (*Mme Gobert*),

Roland Lesaffre (*Roland*), Robert Hébert (*The Doctor*), Louis Péraut (*The Porter*), Colette Régis (*Mother Superior*), Yvonne De Bray (*Old Lady in train*), Claude Borelli (*Lola*), Claude Hennessy, Colette Fleury, Mel Martin, Adeline Aucoc, Alain Nobis, Marcel Arnal, Louise Nowa, Françoise Alban, Paul Temps, Lucienne Juillet.

Filmed on location in Cannes and Paris, and at the Studios Billancourt, February–March 1953. First shown in Paris, 11 November 1953. Running time: 104 min.

Bob le Flambeur (1955)

Production Company	O.G.C./Studios Jenner/Play Art/La Cyme
Producer	Jean-Pierre Melville
Production Manager	Florence Melville
Director	Jean-Pierre Melville
Assistant Directors	François Gir, Guy Aurey, Yves-André Hubert
Script	Jean-Pierre Melville
Dialogue	Auguste Lebreton
Commentary	Written and spoken by Jean-Pierre Melville
Director of Photography	Henri Decaë
Camera Operator	Maurice Blettery
Editor	Monique Bonnot
Art Directors	Jean-Pierre Melville, Claude Bouxin
Music	Eddie Barclay, Jean Boyer
Sound	Pierre Philippenko, Jacques Carrère

Isabelle Corey (*Anne*), Roger Duchesne (*Bob Montagné*), Daniel Cauchy (*Paulo*), Guy Decomble (*The Inspector*), André Garret (*Roger*), Claude Cerval (*Jean*), Colette Fleury (*Jean's wife*), Gérard Buhr (*Marc*), Simone Paris (*Yvonne*), Howard Vernon (*McKimmie*), Germaine Licht (*The Concierge*), Durieux, Jean-Marie Rivière, Kris Kersen, Alleaume, Cichi, Emile Cuvelier (*Gangsters*), Roland Charbeaux, René Havard, Couty, François Gir, Jean-François Drach (*Policemen*), Annick Bertrand (*First Girl in Bar*), Yannick Arvel (*Second Girl in Bar*), Yvette Amirante (*Anne's friend*), André (*Director of the Casino*), Tetelman (*Croupier*), Jean-Marie Robain, and the voices of Henri Decaë and Jean Rossignol.

Filmed on location in Paris and Deauville, and at the Studios Jenner, May–September 1955. First shown in Paris, 24 August 1956. Running time: 100 min.

Deux Hommes dans Manhattan (1958)

Production Company	O.G.C./Alter Films
Producer	Jean-Pierre Melville
Production Managers	Florence Melville, Raymond Blondy
Director	Jean-Pierre Melville
Assistant Directors	Yannick Andrei, Charles Bitsch
Script	Jean-Pierre Melville

Directors of Photography	Nicolas Hayer; Jean-Pierre Melville (New York sequences)
Camera Operators	Jacques Lang, Charles Bitsch, Mike Shrayer, François Reichenbach
Editor	Monique Bonnot
Art Director	Daniel Guéret
Music	Christian Chevallier, Martial Solal
Sound	Jacques Gallois, Jacques Carrère

Pierre Grasset (*Delmas*), Jean-Pierre Melville (*Moreau*), Christiane Eudès (*Anne*), Ginger Hall (*Judith*), Monique Hennessy (*Gloria*), Jean Darcante (*Rouvier*), Jerry Mengo (*McKimmie*), Colette Fleury (*Françoise*), Glenda Leigh (*Virginia*), Jean Lara (*Aubert*), Michèle Bally (*Bessie*), Paula Dehelly (*Mme Fèvre-Berthier*), Carl Studer (*Policeman*), Gloria Kayser (*First Girl*), Darras (*The Drunk*), Bernard Hulin (*Trumpeter*), Yanovitz (*Doorman at Mercury Theatre*), Billy Beck (*Colonel Davidson*), Tetelman (*Bartender*), Art Simmons (*Pianist*), Nancy Delorme, Maurice Pons.

Filmed on location in New York, and at the Studios Jenner and Billancourt, November 1958–April 1959. First shown in Paris, 16 October 1959. Running time: 84 min.

Léon Morin, Prêtre (1961)

Production Company	Rome-Paris Films/C.C. Champion (Rome)
Producers	Carlo Ponti, Georges de Beauregard
Production Manager	Bruna Drigo
Director	Jean-Pierre Melville
Assistant Directors	Luc Andrieux, Volker Schlöndorff, Jacqueline Parey
Script	Jean-Pierre Melville. Based on the novel by Béatrix Beck
Director of Photography	Henri Decaë
Camera Operator	Jean Rabier
Editors	Jacqueline Meppiel, Nadine Marquand, Marie-Josephe Yoyotte, Denise de Casabianca, Agnès Guillemot
Art Directors	Daniel Guéret, Donald Cardwell
Music	Martial Solal, Albert Raisner
Titles	Jean Fouchet
Sound	Guy Villette

Jean-Paul Belmondo (*Léon Morin*), Emmanuelle Riva (*Barny*), Irène Tunc (*Christine Sangredin*), Marielle and Patricia Gozzi (*France*), Nicole Mirel (*Sabine Lévy*), Monique Bertho (*Marion*), Marco Béhar (*Edelman*), Monique Hennessy (*Arlette*), Edith Loria (*Danièlle Holdenberg*), Ernest Varial (*Managing Director*), Nelly Pitorre, Simone Vannier, Lucienne Lemarchand (*The Secretaries*), Madeleine Ganne (*Betty*), Adeline Aucoc (*Old Lady in Church*), Saint-Eve (*The Curé*), Volker Schlöndorff (*The German Sentry*), Gisèle Grimm (*Lucienne*), Howard Vernon (*The Colonel*), Gérard Buhr (*German Soldier*), Cedric Grant.

Filmed on location at Grenoble, and at the Studios Jenner, January–March 1961.
First shown in Paris, 22 September 1961 (previously at the Venice Film Festival, out
of competition, 3 September 1961). Running time: 128 min.

Le Doulos (1962)

Production Company	Rome-Paris Films/C.C. Champion (Rome)
Producers	Carlo Ponti, Georges de Beauregard
Director	Jean-Pierre Melville
Assistant Directors	Volker Schlöndorff, Charles Bitsch
Script	Jean-Pierre Melville. Based on the novel by Pierre Lesou
Director of Photography	Nicolas Hayer
Camera Operator	Henri Tiquet
Editors	Monique Bonnot, Michèle Boehm
Art Director	Daniel Guéret
Music	Paul Misraki; piano music, Jacques Loussier
Sound	Julien Coutellier

Jean-Paul Belmondo (*Silien*), Serge Reggiani (*Maurice Faugel*), Jean Desailly
(*Inspector Clain*), Fabienne Dali (*Fabienne*), Michel Piccoli (*Nuttheccio*), René
Lefèvre (*Gilbert Varnove*), Marcel Cuvelier (*First Detective*), Jack Léonard (*Second
Detective*), Aimé de March (*Jean*), Monique Hennessy (*Thérèse*), Carl Studer (*Kern*),
Christian Lude (*The Doctor*), Jacques de Léon (*Armand*), Paulette Breil (*Anita*),
Philippe Nahon (*Rémy*), Charles Bayard (*Old Man*), Daniel Crohem (*Inspector
Salignari*), Charles Bouillaud (*Barman*), Georges Sellier (*Barman*), Andrès (*Maître
d'hôtel*).

Filmed on location in Paris and at the Studios Jenner, April–June 1962. First shown
in Paris, 8 February 1963. Running time: 108 min.

L'Ainé des Ferchaux (1962)

Production Company	Fernand Lumbroso (Paris)/Ultra Films (Rome)
Producer	Fernand Lumbroso
Production Managers	Jérôme Sutter, Jean Darvey
Director	Jean-Pierre Melville
Assistant Directors	Yves Boisset, Georges Pellegrin
Script	Jean-Pierre Melville. Based on the novel by Georges Simenon
Director of Photography	Henri Decaë (Franscope)
Camera Operator	Alain Douarinou
Colour Process	Eastman Colour
Editors	Monique Bonnot, Claude Durand
Art Director	Daniel Guéret
Music	Georges Delerue
Sound	Julien Coutellier, Jean-Claude Marchetti

Jean-Paul Belmondo (*Michel Maudet*), Charles Vanel (*Dieudonné Ferchaux*), Michèle Mercier (*Lou*), Malvina (*Lina*), Stefania Sandrelli (*The Hitch-hiker*), Todd Martin (*Jeff*), E.-F. Médard (*Suska*), Jerry Mengo (*The Banker*), Andrex (*M. Andrei*), André Certes (*Emile Ferchaux*), Barbara Sommers (*Lou's friend*), Delia Kent (*Prostitute*), Hugues Wanner, Paul Sorrèze, Charles Bayard, Pierre Leproux, Zeller (*Board members*), Simone Darot, Ginger Hall.

Filmed on location in France and America, and at the Studios Jenner, August–November 1962. First shown in Paris, 2 October 1963 (previously at New York Film Festival, 17 September 1963). Running time: 102 min.

Le Deuxième Souffle (1966)

Production Company	Les Productions Montaigne/Charles Lumbroso
Producers	Charles Lumbroso, André Labay
Production Manager	Alain Quéffélean
Director	Jean-Pierre Melville
Assistant Directors	Jean-François Adam, Georges Pellegrin
Script	Jean-Pierre Melville. Based on the novel by José Giovanni
Dialogue	Jean-Pierre Melville, José Giovanni
Director of Photography	Marcel Combes
Camera Operator	Jean Charvein
Editor	Michel Boehm
Art Director	Jean-Jacques Fabre
Music	Bernard Gérard
Sound	Jacques Gallois

Lino Ventura (*Gustave Minda*), Paul Meurisse (*Inspector Blot*), Raymond Pellegrin (*Paul Ricci*), Christine Fabrega (*Manouche*), Pierre Zimmer (*Orloff*), Michel Constantin (*Alban*), Marcel Bozzufi (*Jo Ricci*), Paul Frankeur (*Inspector Fardiano*), Denis Manuel (*Antoine*), Pierre Grasset (*Pascal Léonetti*), Jean Négroni (*Policeman*), Raymond Loyer (*Jacques-le-Notaire*), Albert Dagnant (*Jeannot Franchi*), Jean-Claude Bercq, Régis Outin, Jack Léonard, Albert Michel, Nina Michaelsen, Betty Anglade.

Filmed on location in Paris and Marseilles, and at the Studios Jenner, February–March, June–August 1966. First shown in Paris, 2 November 1966. Running time: 150 min.

Le Samourai (1967)

Production Company	Filmel/C.I.C.C. (Paris)/Fida Cinematografica (Rome)
Producer	Eugène Lépicier
Production Manager	Georges Casati
Director	Jean-Pierre Melville
Assistant Director	Georges Pellegrin
Script	Jean-Pierre Melville.

173

Director of Photography	Henri Decaë
Camera Operator	Jean Charvein
Colour Process	Eastman Colour
Editors	Monique Bonnot, Yolande Maurette
Art Director	François de Lamothe; assistant, Théo Meurisse
Music	François de Roubaix
Sound	René Longuet

Alain Delon (*Jeff Costello*), Nathalie Delon (*Jeanne Lagrange*), François Périer (*The Inspector*), Cathy Rosier (*Valérie*), Jacques Leroy (*The Gunman*), Jean-Pierre Posier (*Olivier Rey*), Catherine Jourdan (*Hatcheck Girl*), Michel Boisrond (*Wiener*), Robert Favart (*The Barman*), Carlo Nell, Roger Fradet, André Thorent, Carl Lechner, Pierre Vander, Georges Casati.

Filmed on location in Paris and at the Studios Jenner and Saint-Maurice, June–August 1967. First shown in Paris, 25 October 1967. Running time: 95 min.

L'Armée des Ombres (1969)

Production Company	Corona (Paris)/Fono Roma (Rome)
Producer	Robert Dorfmann
Executive Producer	Jacques Dorfmann
Director	Jean-Pierre Melville
Assistant Directors	Jean-François Adam, Georges Pellegrin
Script	Jean-Pierre Melville. Based on the novel by Joseph Kessel
Director of Photography	Pierre Lhomme
Colour Process	Eastman Colour
Editor	Françoise Bonnot
Art Director	Théo Meurisse
Music	Eric de Marsan
Sound	Jean Nény

Lino Ventura (*Philippe Gerbier*), Paul Meurisse (*Luc Jardie*), Simone Signoret (*Mathilde*), Jean-Pierre Cassel (*Jean-François*), Claude Mann (*Le Masque*), Christian Barbier (*Le Bison*), Serge Reggiani (*The Barber*), Alain Libolt (*The Traitor*), Paul Crauchet (*Felix*), Alain Mottet (*Commandant of Camp*), Jean-Marie Robain, André Dewawrin, Alain Decok, Albert Michel, Henri Daquin, Marco Perrin, Michel Fretault, Gérard Huart, Denis Sadier.

Filmed on location in France and at the Studios Boulogne, January–March 1969. First shown in Paris, 12 September 1969. Running time: 140 min.

Le Cercle Rouge (1970)

Production Company	Corona (Paris)/Selenia (Rome)
Producer	Robert Dorfmann
Production Manager	Jean-Pierre Melville
Director	Jean-Pierre Melville
Assistant Director	Bernard Stora
Script	Jean-Pierre Melville
Director of Photography	Henri Decaë
Camera Operator	Charles-Henri Montel
Colour Process	Eastman Colour
Art Director	Théo Meurisse
Music	Eric de Marsan
Sound	Jean Nény

Alain Delon (*Corey*), André Bourvil (*Commissaire Mattei*), Yves Montand (*Jansen*), François Périer (*Santi*), Gian Maria Volonté (*Vogel*), André Eykan (*Rico*), Pierre Collet (*Prison Warder*), Paul Crauchet (*The Fence*), Paul Amiot (*Inspecteur Général des Services*), Jean-Pierre Posier (*Matteï's assistant*), Jean-Marc Boris (*Santi's son*).

Filmed on location in and around Paris, Chalon-sur-Saône, Marseilles, and at the Studios Boulogne, January–April 1970.

Short Film

Vingt Quatre Heures de la Vie d'un Clown (1946)

Production Company	Melville Productions
Producer	Jean-Pierre Melville
Director	Jean-Pierre Melville
Script	Jean-Pierre Melville
Assistant Directors	Carlos Villardebo, Michel Clément
Directors of Photography	Gustave Raulet, André Villard
Editor	Monique Bonnot
Music	Maïs, Cassel

With: Bèby, Maïs.
Running time: 22 min.

Melville played a leading role in his own *Deux Hommes dans Manhattan* (1958), and has also appeared in small parts in the following films: *Les Drames du Bois de Boulogne* (Jacques Loew, 1948), *Orphée* (Jean Cocteau, 1949; as the Hotel Manager), *Un Amour de Poche* (Pierre Kast, 1957; as the Police Commissioner), *A Bout de Souffle* (Jean-Luc Godard, 1959; as the novelist Parvulesco), and *Landru* (Claude Chabrol, 1962; as Georges Mandel).

Bourvil as Inspector Mattëi in *Le Cercle Rouge* (with Melville's three cats – Griffaulait, Fiorello and Aufrène)

Acknowledgements

Stills by courtesy of André Dino, the F.F.C.C. (Fédération Française des Ciné-Clubs), The National Film Archive, Henry Moret; Jean-Pierre Labret and his secretary Mme. Ginestou . . . and Jean-Pierre Melville.

The author would like to thank Tom Milne who did the translation and made many helpful suggestions; Nicoletta Zalaffi who read and re-read and gave all kinds of advice; David Meeker who arranged the only screening I had of *Léon Morin, Prêtre*; Henry Moret who completed the filmography; Penelope Houston, Gillian Hartnoll, Jan Dawson and Sylvia Loeb for their great help; Christine Guimard, Jean-Bernard and Janine Pouy, Monique Griboval, Jean-Pierre and Pierrette Fleutiaux . . . and lastly Jean-Pierre Melville who took a sizeable amount of time off his heavy work schedule during the editing of *L'Armée des Ombres* and the shooting of *Le Cercle Rouge* to do these interviews.

This book is for my father and mother, José and Laurentina Nogueira, qui m'ont toujours permis de vivre à ma guise . . .

   . . . and for . . .

Nicoletta Zalaffi, my wife.